British Defence

A Blueprint for Reform

Also available from Brassey's

CARTWRIGHT & CRITCHLEY
Cruise, Pershing & SS-20

COKER
A Nation in Retreat? Britain's Defence Commitment

COKER
British Defence in the 1990s: A Guide to the Defence Debate

MCINNES
Trident: The Only Option?

RAMSBOTHAM
Choices: Nuclear and Non-Nuclear Defence Options

WINDASS
The Rite of War

British Defence
A Blueprint for Reform

by

MICHAEL CHICHESTER

and

JOHN WILKINSON

BRASSEY'S DEFENCE PUBLISHERS
(a member of the Pergamon Group)

LONDON · OXFORD · WASHINGTON · NEW YORK
BEIJING · FRANKFURT · SAO PAULO · SYDNEY · TOKYO · TORONTO

U.K. (Editorial)	Brassey's Defence Publishers, 24 Gray's Inn Road, London WC1X 8HR
(Orders)	Brassey's Defence Publishers, Headington Hill Hall, Oxford OX3 0BW, England
U.S.A. (Editorial)	Pergamon-Brassey's International Defense Publishers, 8000 Westpark Drive, Fourth Floor McLean, Virginia 22101, U.S.A.
(Orders)	Pergamon Press, Maxwell House, Fairview Park, Elmsford, New York 10523, U.S.A.
PEOPLE'S REPUBLIC OF CHINA	Pergamon Press, Room 4037, Qianmen Hotel, Beijing, People's Republic of China
FEDERAL REPUBLIC OF GERMANY	Pergamon Press, Hammerweg 6, D-6242 Kronberg, Federal Republic of Germany
BRAZIL	Pergamon Editora, Rua Eça de Queiros, 346, CEP 04011, Paraiso, São Paulo, Brazil
AUSTRALIA	Pergamon-Brassey's Defence Publishers, P.O. Box 544, Potts Point, N.S.W. 2011, Australia
JAPAN	Pergamon Press, 8th Floor, Matsuoka Central Building, 1-7-1 Nishishinjuku, Shinjuku-ku, Tokyo 160, Japan
CANADA	Pergamon Press Canada, Suite No. 271, 253 College Street, Toronto, Ontario, Canada M5T 1R5

First edition 1987

Library of Congress Cataloging in Publication Data

Chichester, Michael, 1917–
British Defence.
1. Great Britain——Military policy. 2. Great Britain—
Armed Forces. I. Wilkinson, John, 1940–
II. Title.
UA647.C553 1987 355′.0335′41 87-10377

British Library Cataloguing in Publication Data

Chichester, Michael
British Defence: a blueprint for reform.
1. Great Britain——Military policy
I. Title II. Wilkinson, John, 1940–
355′.0335′41 UA647

ISBN 0-08-034745-2

Printed and bound in Great Britain by
Redwood Burn Limited, Trowbridge, Wiltshire

"Now, brethren, if I come unto you speaking with tongues, what shall I profit you, except I shall speak to you either by revelation, or by knowledge, or by prophesying, or by doctrine?

And even things without life giving sound, whether pipe or harp, except they give a distinction in the sounds, how shall it be known what is piped or harped? For if the trumpet give an uncertain sound, who shall prepare himself to the battle?"

First Epistle of St. Paul to the Corinthians, Chapter XIV, vv. 6–9

The opinions expressed in this book are of the authors only and not of any Party or Organisation.

Foreword

by Admiral of the Fleet Lord Lewin, KG, GCB, LVO, DSC

THIS is a timely book, coming as it does when the bipartisan approach which has so long been the basis of UK Defence Policy has been abandoned, when the outlook for an agreed reduction in nuclear weapons seems bright and when we are in the run up to elections in both the United Kingdom and the United States. In the background is the realisation that we have now enjoyed more than forty years of peace in Europe; an increasing proportion of the electorate perhaps considers this to be the natural state of international relations, not one that needs to be watched, guarded and insured by the payment of an adequate premium if it is to be preserved. Democratic pressures have obliged even a Conservative Government committed to maintaining our security to set future defence expenditure on a plateau, which in fact means a reduction in real terms. It is an opportune time to review the past, examine the present and look ahead to the future.

Michael Chichester and John Wilkinson set out the factors and events that have influenced the development of our Defence Policy over the last twenty years. During that time I had seven appointments in Whitehall, all connected with the formulation of defence policy and I can vouch for the accuracy of their account. They reach the conclusion that some change in strategic priorities is now inevitable and indicate a new direction for NATO and for the United Kingdom contribution to the Alliance. There is much here with which I would agree, particularly the need for NATO to consider its position in a world which has changed almost beyond recognition since 1954, to reassess both the contribution it could best make to international security and the contribution that the individual members could best make to the Alliance.

Closer to home I applaud their emphasis on the need for a "Defence" approach to United Kingdom strategic problems; the strengthened position of the Chief of the Defence Staff and those who serve him will help to achieve this. Inter-service rivalry is dangerously counter-productive, modern warfare is a combined operation, none can manage without the other. To this end I would put the amalgamation of the three service Staff Colleges well before the linking of young officer training which the authors recommend – and much easier to achieve.

This book should stimulate a better informed and much needed discussion on the future direction of British Defence Policy. I hope it will be widely read, but most important I hope it will be marked and inwardly digested by the Secretary of State for Defence in the next Administration, whoever that may be. To him may fall the task of translating the blueprint into reality.

Lewin

Acknowledgements

The authors wish to express their grateful thanks to Jill Toedtli for her patient and painstaking typing of the manuscript, and for the kind assistance of Virginia Hope

The Authors

Michael Chichester was educated at the Royal Naval College, Dartmouth, and served in the Royal Navy until 1961 when he retired in the rank of Commander.

During the Second World War he saw service at sea in the Home Fleet and in the Western Approaches Command. In 1955–56 he commanded the destroyer, HMS *Contest*.

On leaving the Royal Navy he entered the City. Since his retirement from the Service he has maintained a keen interest in British defence and strategic policy. From 1962 to 1967 he was Defence Correspondent of the weekly *Statist*. For some fifteen years he contributed regular articles on current defence affairs to the monthly magazine *Navy* (now *Navy International*).

In 1982 with John Wilkinson he published *The Uncertain Ally – British Defence Policy, 1960–1990*.

John Wilkinson has served as Conservative Member of Parliament for Ruislip-Northwood since 1979 and was MP for Bradford West from 1970 to 1974.

He was educated at Eton (King's Scholar), the Royal Air Force College, Cranwell, and Churchill College, Cambridge.

He served as a flying instructor in the Royal Air Force and was Personal Assistant to the Chairman of the British Aircraft Corporation.

John Wilkinson is a former Chairman of the Conservative Party Aviation Committee and former Vice-Chairman of the Conservative Defence Committee.

He was Parliamentary Private Secretary to the Secretary of State for Defence, Sir John Nott, during the Falklands War. He is Chairman of the Committee on Scientific, Technological and Aerospace Questions of Western European Union and of the Space Sub Committees both of the Conservative Party in the House of Commons and of the Council of Europe.

In addition to *The Uncertain Ally*, he has written and lectured extensively in the fields of Defence and Strategic Studies.

Contents

List of Tables

Preface

THE state of a nation's defence and the importance a nation accords to the profession of arms are good indications of its self esteem and the worth it attaches to its society. In a democracy this is particularly true. A country's security and military strength are assured first by a strong popular commitment to democracy itself and secondly by a firm political will on the part of elected representatives to ensure that in spite of more electorally attractive competing priorities the means are voted to assure the preservation of national sovereignty and independence.

In Britain today there is wide disinterest in defence. Reliance on all-regular forces insulates the majority of the population from the personal sacrifice and burdens of bearing arms. The absence of conscription means that most people have no conception of military service as a dimension of citizenship. The passage of two generations since World War II and one generation since the end of National Service renders dim the folk memory of war and conflict and the discipline of military life.

Illusions persist in Britain about the realities of the global balance of power and the direct physical threats to British independence and democratic liberties posed by the Soviet Union and its Allies. It is all too readily assumed that the professionalism of the United Kingdom Armed Forces will compensate for their small numbers. Supposedly the assurance of collective security enshrined in the NATO Alliance will make up for the deficiencies of Britain's purely national defence efforts and the United States' nuclear guarantee will deter Soviet aggression triggered if necessary by Britain's independent nuclear deterrent, regardless of the inadequacies of Western Europe's conventional forces. Wishful thinking is the supreme characteristic of Britain's defence strategy today. Complacency and indifference are the hallmarks of the security policies of Western Europe as a whole.

For Britain the transition in the space of twenty years from global responsibilities underpinned by military power sustained by a worldwide chain of bases and the means of long-range power projection has not been easy. The abandonment of a post imperial global posture in favour of a primarily European role centred on the North Atlantic Treaty area was accompanied by a series of low intensity operations in Kenya, Cyprus, Malaysia, Oman, Aden, and latterly Northern Ireland.

Surprisingly the United Kingdom has concentrated less on those fields of military operation in which a direct experience was obtained, notably counter insurgency and anti-guerrilla warfare than on maintaining the pretensions of Continental power in Europe. The Brussels Treaty commitment of 55,000 men and a Tactical Air Force on the Continent of Europe, entered into in the heyday of National Service in Britain has been maintained, even though the United Kingdom is the sole country among the Warsaw Pact nations and the European members of NATO to have abandoned conscription.

Primarily for political reasons which will be examined further, the United Kingdom has persisted with a manpower intensive strategy. But the preferred policy to meet the manpower needs of this strategy, a policy unique amongst the European NATO countries, has become more and more expensive with the result that the nation's armed forces have become smaller and smaller over the years. So the ability of all-regular professional forces to compensate through superior equipment, specialisation and training for their lack of numbers has been reduced. This ability has been most impaired in the naval and air forces and in the associated amphibious and air mobile units for long-range intervention.

The innate conservatism of the British defence establishment has considerable merit. The preservation of the elements of the regimental system, much tradition in all three Services and a sense of pageantry associated with ceremonial and Royal occasions are undoubtedly sources of pride and foster positive morale. The successful outcome of the Falklands War owed at least as much to the personal qualities and fighting spirit of individual units as to the quality of the equipment of the British servicemen involved.

Yet this conservatism also has profoundly negative consequences. The political necessity of maintaining an outward and visible sign of the United Kingdom's commitment to the security of the Federal Republic of Germany by means of a British military presence on its soil has created a Maginot Line mentality which forbids even asking the question whether the British forces in Germany, particularly the British Army of the Rhine, with all their attendant impedimenta of expensive civilian support, married quarters, NAAFI shops, schools and swimming pools are the best way of fulfilling this commitment. The balance between British defence assets vested in a single static role on the central front of continental Europe and those available for flexible and mobile application elsewhere has moved steadily in favour of the continental role despite the fact that Soviet military power has grown worldwide and the threat to Western interests outside the NATO area has increased.

There is a disturbing lack of innovative strategic thinking in the United Kingdom both in Government and Parliament. Within the Services also attitudes have ossified. The Army, where thinking is often dominated by generals whose formative years were spent in peacetime soldiering on the

North German plain, has been extraordinarily slow to exploit the tactical potential of the helicopter. The belief has continued that the best antidote to armour remains the main battle tank, even though the combination of airpower and intelligent guided weapons offers hitherto unimagined opportunities for NATO forces to counter the armoured preponderance of the Warsaw Pact.

For the United Kingdom supremacy at sea has for long been the cornerstone of national security. However, since World War II Britain's maritime power has steadily declined. The Royal Navy today is very much the poor relation of the three Services, even though, since the Nassau agreement of 1962, its responsibility for Britain's independent nuclear deterrent force, through the Polaris submarine-launched ballistic missile system due to be replaced soon by the similar but more powerful Trident D5 system has assured it a key but controversial role in Britain's national security.

Nevertheless over the years the Royal Navy has been the victim of savage retrenchment primarily imposed by politicians. The abandonment of large aircraft carriers with a strike capability has been only very partially offset by the introduction into service of the INVINCIBLE class of small carriers, originally designated "through deck cruisers", with a primary role of anti-submarine warfare (ASW).

The size of Britain's surface fleet is now barely adequate to maintain the important contribution to NATO's ASW and escort forces in the Eastern Atlantic and Channel command areas upon which the Western Alliance has relied for so long. Naval reserves are pitifully weak and dwindling in number. The catastrophic contraction in the size of Britain's merchant navy continues. If it is allowed to go any further there will be virtually no merchant shipping under the British flag left to be drawn upon in an emergency.

Despite having had to relinquish its role as the custodian of Britain's independent strategic nuclear deterrent force when the switch to a submarine-based system was made, the Royal Air Force still operates on the assumption of a short war. In this it is not unique since the weaknesses of NATO conventional forces as a whole are bound to put a premium on NATO's invoking at least a tactical nuclear response to Warsaw Pact advances relatively early in the event of any conflict in Europe. Unlike the Army, however, the Royal Air Force has virtually no reserves at all either of men or of aircraft.

Losses for NATO Air Forces, particularly in Northern and Central Europe, are likely to be extremely high. They will be even higher if the Warsaw Pact enjoys the benefits of surprise. Yet the sustainability of the Royal Air Force is minimal. All its main assets are in the front line and lacking auxiliary squadrons the RAF's main means of making good attrition is by denuding the conversion units which are essential for the supply of new pilots. The RAF continues to undervalue the lessons of those Air Forces with recent operational experience from the Near East and Viet

Nam conflicts, namely those of Israel and the United States, that reserve crews are essential to augment the front line and can operate to exactly the same standards as their regular counterparts.

It would be wrong to blame the Armed Forces alone for the deficiencies of Britain's defences. Successive Governments, an ill-informed Parliament and a disinterested public are at least equally to blame. Above all, the essential consensus between the main political parties on British defence and security policy has broken down. The activities of CND and the peace movements, aided and abetted primarily by the Labour Party and by large elements of the Liberal Party, have undermined public confidence in nuclear deterrence as a whole. Britain's role as an independent nuclear power and the long-term viability of the US nuclear guarantee are now in question.

As the values and priorities of the Conservative Party and the Labour Party diverge further in the face of increasing pacifist and neutralist inroads into the Labour movement, the future alignment of British Foreign Policy becomes more doubtful. It is hard to judge whether the gullible, wishful thinkers who equate the deeds and motives of the two superpowers are the victims of disinformation or wilful ignorance. The United States' actions such as the invasion of Grenada, the air raids against terrorist bases in Libya, or attempts to check the Sandinista revolution in Nicaragua are often criticised more than the Soviet invasion and occupation of Afghanistan and Soviet support for brutal and bloody Marxist régimes like those in Ethiopia and Angola. The effect is the same – increasing calls from the Left for the closure of US nuclear bases in Britain that have their echoes among West Germany's Socialists and cause a steady disintegration of the political unity of the Western Alliance which is the ultimate guarantor of Western Europe's liberty and independence.

To political uncertainty and division must be added the ever dominant influence of Britain's economic impoverishment and decline. The NATO target of a three per cent increase in defence spending in real terms was maintained by Britain, not until the Soviet threat had been matched, but until the electoral prospects of the Conservative Party looked so alarming that Mrs. Thatcher's Government felt obliged to yield to the voters' clamour for more popular spending programmes like health, education, housing and welfare. In as much as on its public pledges an incoming Socialist Government would do much more damage to Britain's defences than any amount of Conservative retrenchment on defence, this was justifiable policy in political terms, but in military terms it was not.

Since Duncan Sandys' White Paper of 1957, British Defence Policy has been guided more by economic than by military considerations. Each successive defence "review" has been impelled by an urgent necessity to save money rather than by any convincing demonstration of strategic foresight, or by any objective appraisal of the changing needs of national security and of the most suitable British contribution to the containment of the Soviet global threat.

Throughout its post-war history, the evolution of the defence and strategic policies of the United Kingdom has been dominated by certain recurring themes of which the need to adjust to the exigencies imposed by declining economic strength has been the most frequent and the most influential. The continuing debate between those who advocate a "continental" and those who argue the merits of a "maritime" strategy, doubts about the necessity of overseas military commitments, and the degree of "out of Area" capability that should be maintained are other examples of these themes.

Equipment procurement policy remains controversial, as the Westland and the Nimrod AEW episodes demonstrated. The extent to which collaborative programmes can be carried out amongst the NATO European nations, how far a two-way street between the USA and Europe in defence equipment is possible, the benefits of standardisation and interoperability within the Alliance; all these are the subject of many learned papers and much debate, but all too little practical progress.

Manpower policies, too, can no longer be ignored. The accepted wisdom that all regular wholly volunteer forces suit Britain best now has to be questioned. In particular, if the country's foreign policy continues to require the maintenance of the Brussels Treaty commitment to station 55,000 troops and a Tactical Air Force on the continent of Europe, a new manpower policy for the armed forces will be needed to prevent a further degree of imbalance in the structure of the Services. There are compelling arguments in favour of such new manpower policies in addition to the purely military ones.

In an era of high unemployment, and widespread youth alienation and violence, is there not a social role for Britain's armed forces in making her young people better citizens whilst at the same time giving them the opportunity of active participation in the defence of their country? Reliance on "indigenous mercenaries" may be convenient for the services themselves, but is the growing lack of contact between the military and the civilian elements of society beneficial for either? Should the reintroduction of National Service remain a political taboo and why cannot the many and varied skills of the civilian community be more effectively mobilised for national defence?

Matters such as the higher structure of the armed forces and the role and responsibilities of the Chiefs of Staff within the Ministry of Defence are perennial sources of interest to the connoisseur, as are the education and training of military officers. But the parliamentary monitoring of defence policy and its political presentation to the public at large both need to be improved. The creation of a political constituency within Western Europe as a whole to enhance the co-ordination of arms collaboration and security policy generally amongst the European members of NATO may seem subjects fit only for specialist debate, but their importance is greater than is often realised.

Above all, a reinvigoration of the NATO Alliance is long overdue. A re-examination of its strategy and a new concertation of its policy, at least amongst its leading members, has become essential to its continuing effectiveness. Britain's role as a maritime nation to the rear and on the flank of continental Europe with considerable overseas interests of its own; the natural bridge for reinforcements from the USA for Western Europe; the marshalling point for air and amphibious forces; all these factors need to be reviewed in a comprehensive analysis of how to make better use of the resources of the Western Alliance as a whole for its common defence.

Such a re-examination of roles and responsibilities within the NATO Alliance has to be undertaken at a time when Britain's American friends are themselves having to reduce their defence appropriations to limit the size of the US budget deficit. American security preoccupations are directed increasingly towards the Pacific Basin for strategic as well as commercial considerations and towards Latin America more and more in order to check the expansion of Marxist orientated movements, such as the Sandinistas in Nicaragua. In these circumstances public and political opinion in the United States needs to be satisfied that its NATO allies in Europe are assuming a fair share of the burden of the Alliance's common defence.

This book will address all these issues. It is bound to be controversial. It is meant to be. The disinterest in Britain's defence policy born of benign neglect of some of the most challenging issues in UK security policy is almost as dangerous as the sloganeering and simplistic prescriptions of the anti-nuclear and anti-American lobbies. Jargon and technical terminology will be avoided as much as possible. The dangers of perpetuating weak national defences are worthy of serious consideration by the general reader and not just by the specialist defence expert. If popular interest in these matters can be aroused, the effort will have been vindicated.

CHAPTER I

The Mirage of Power and the Reality of Penury

The Economic Constraints on British Defence Policy

The Attlee Years. The Founding of Britain's Post-War Defence Policy

In the years immediately following the end of World War II, the Labour Government of Clement Attlee determined to maintain the position of power and influence in world affairs which Britain had achieved by its leading role in the war and in the peace negotiations which followed. Britain was still a great power, one of the "Big Three", and her substantial military strength deployed almost world-wide was to play an essential part in the restoration of stability and security not only in the overseas areas for which she retained responsibility but in many parts of Western Europe as well. Two years after VE Day Britain still had over 1¼ million men and women in the armed forces.

By then the unco-operative and hostile attitude of Soviet Russia towards her former allies, particularly over the reconstruction of Europe, had become clear; almost exactly one year after VE Day, on 3 May 1946, Ernest Bevin, the Foreign Secretary, gave the Cabinet his opinion that "*The danger of Russia has become certainly as great as and possibly even greater than, a revived Germany.*"[1] Thereafter events moved quickly as the geo-strategic pattern of Europe which exists to this day evolved; in 1947 the announcement of the Marshall Plan, 1948 the Treaty of Brussels in which Britain, France and the Benelux countries bound themselves in a fifty year pact of mutual aid and defence against any aggressor, and, finally, 1949 the signing of the North Atlantic Treaty in the creation of which Bevin had played such an important part.

The Brussels Treaty marked the origins of Britain's post-war commitment to the defence of Western Europe, a commitment subsequently enshrined in the North Atlantic Treaty ensuring the assignment of substantial British forces to NATO commands in war, and confirmed in 1954 by Sir Anthony Eden's pledge to maintain 55,000 British troops and a tactical air force permanently deployed in the Federal Republic of Germany. For Britain the Treaty "*marked a remarkable transformation in foreign policy compared with the previous quiescence towards Western Europe which had endured, largely unbroken, since the end of the Peninsular War in 1812.*"[2]

Forty years on the twin pillars of British defence and strategic policy are the maintenance of an independent strategic nuclear deterrent force committed to the NATO Alliance, and of a substantial multi-role conventional contribution of land, sea, and air forces to the defence of the NATO area. The origins of the Continental commitment have already been described. The Attlee Government was also responsible for the birth of the British nuclear deterrent.

In November 1945, the United States proved unwilling to establish new agreements with Britain and Canada on the exchange of atomic energy information. In August 1946, the passing of the McMahon Act transferred control of atomic energy in America from the military authorities to the civilian Atomic Energy Commission, and forbade transmission of atomic information of any kind to other countries. For the Attlee government this was a political rebuff, the effects of which were deemed to be as serious as those stemming from the ending of Lend Lease. This had made Britain heavily dependent on the generosity of the USA for the financial help needed to repair the ravages of what had proved after all to be a Pyrrhic victory in economic terms.

Deprived of economic independence, the British government feared that Washington's isolationism over atomic energy could threaten its political independence as well. The passing of the McMahon Act showed that co-operation with the USA over the production of the new and devastating weapon – the possession of which was essential to maintain the pretensions of Great Power status – would no longer be possible. In January 1947 advised by the Chiefs of Staff and in great secrecy, Attlee decided that Britain should manufacture her own atomic bombs. The birth of the British independent strategic nuclear deterrent had taken place; Polaris and Trident are its descendents. As Attlee put it at the time:

> "*For a power of our size and with our responsibilities to turn its back on the Bomb did not make sense*".[3]

By the end of 1945 Britain had sold over £1.1 billion of capital assets abroad, had increased her external debt by over £2.8 billion, and had reduced her gold and dollar reserves by £152 million. Recovery of the export trade was essential to pay for the imports needed to improve the standard of living and restore the capacity to manufacture. Yet in 1946 at £1.112 billion British defence expenditure was equal to twenty per cent of the gross national product and although it had been possible to reduce this to £700 million in 1948, it rose again to £780 million as a result of the re-armament programme introduced at the start of the Korean war in June 1950. Given the state of the economy at the end of the war and the crippling cost of victory, the tenacity of the Attlee Government over its insistence on maintaining Britain's position of influence in the emerging post-war world was remarkable.

> *"In general, the Labour administration, with occasional opposition from Dalton and Bevan, accepted the military aspects and financial costs of Britain's status as a great power."*[4]

It was not only in the allocation of scarce financial resources that the costs of military power were in competition with the needs of other vital programmes. Manpower had to be transferred from the forces to begin the huge task of national reconstruction. In June 1945 there had been 5,090,000 men and women in the armed forces and 16.55 million working civilians of whom over forty per cent were engaged on war production. This was a national mobilisation of resources for war higher than in any other allied country.[5]

In August 1950, the Cabinet agreed to substantial British involvement in the defence of South Korea and initiated an expensive re-armament programme. The initial cost of the programme was £3.4 billion from 1951–54; by January 1951, this estimate had risen to £4.7 billion. This was a huge financial burden for the British economy resulting in a higher level of defence spending per capita than that incurred by the people of the USA at the time. Exports would be reduced and manpower transferred back to defence production. National Service was extended from eighteen months to two years and the improvement in living standards halted. But all these consequences were accepted in the interests of aiding the US war effort in Korea.

> *"This transformed defence commitment, into which the Cabinet was stampeded in January 1951, marked a profound watershed in British political history. . . . Its political and financial implications were to dominate British public affairs for a decade to come."*[6]

As the effects of the re-armament programme began to be appreciated, political opposition to it mounted. Aneurin Bevan bitterly disputed the introduction of National Health Service charges during the winter of 1950–51, claiming the re-armament programme made them necessary. A future Prime Minister, then at the Board of Trade, directed some barbed shafts at his colleagues on the economic consequences of this programme, particularly over the effects on the balance of payments and the strength of sterling. The era of fixed exchange rates was then in force and fears of another devaluation against the dollar constantly haunted ministers.

Both Bevan and Wilson resigned from the Government in April 1951. Thereafter the economic situation continued to worsen. Increased defence production reduced the earnings from manufactured exports resulting in a growing deterioration in the balance of payments as Wilson had forecast.

The opening shots of the long battle of Weapons versus Welfare had been fired. In very different circumstances the engagement was still in progress thirty-five years later having endured in a desultory fashion throughout the intervening years; indeed, there is no reason to suppose that an armistice will be reached, let alone peace declared, for the foreseeable future.

In the general election of October 1951, the Conservatives were returned to power and lost no time in "reviewing" the re-armament programme. Winston Churchill, once more Prime Minister, admitted to the Commons that the 1951–52 defence budget of £1.250 billion could not be afforded in the deteriorating economic circumstances. Defence spending was severely curtailed and the costs of the original programme spread over a longer period. Salami slicing had begun.

Attlee's over-ambitious re-armament programme of 1950–51 had contributed to the downfall of his administration and to the series of corrective measures which marked the subsequent thirteen "wasted" years of Conservative rule, the initial cuts in defence spending following the 1951 general election, the post-Suez defence review of Duncan Sandys in 1957, and the ending of military national service in 1962. In the end, even these proved insufficient to match the continuing weakness of the British economy.

What lessons can be drawn from this story of the economic and political background to the origins of the twin pillars of post-war British defence policy and of Attlee's courageous attempts to keep Britain a great power?

The emerging threat of Soviet imperialism wherever manifest (Berlin, Korea) was recognised and the need to maintain a military capacity appropriate to Great Power status to face this threat accepted with little hesitation or argument. The political will overcame the considerable economic case which could be mounted against such a posture. But in the end the realities of the country's economic weakness revealed the inability of Britain to devote more than a certain level of its national product to defence without dangerously weakening the country's balance of payments and hence its currency and, in the aftermath of war, without delaying the restoration of its civil economy and of the standard of living of its people. Forty years on these effects of a high level of defence spending have largely disappeared but they have been replaced by others, equally constraining.

1955–75. The Philosophy of the Short War and the Withdrawal into Europe

The second post war decade began with the Suez operation and ended with Harold Wilson's newly elected Labour Government preparing its first defence review. Suez had been one of the causes of the 1957 defence review which had been largely brought about by the realisation that in the emerging world of the super powers Britain could no longer "go it alone" on the international stage, either politically or economically without at least the tacit support of Washington.

This review was the first post war attempt to define a defence policy which the country could afford and which endeavoured to foresee the role of conventional forces in the thermo-nuclear age which was just beginning. To the extent that it combined economic realism with a broad brush forecast of the strategic future (e.g. "*The role of naval forces in total war is somewhat uncertain*,"[7] it was more honest than some of its successors in which specific strategic doctrines of doubtful validity were propounded to justify particular reductions in military capabilities which in turn would produce the defence "cuts" demanded at the time, (1966, 1981). But in facing up to the dilemma posed by the devastating power of the new generation of nuclear weapons it accepted without argument a concept for British defence and strategic policy first adumbrated by Harold Macmillan (later Earl of Stockton) in the 1955 Defence White Paper – the philosophy of the "Short War".

In his opinion Europe could only be defended against "the massive preponderance" of Soviet and Warsaw Pact satellite armies by the use of nuclear weapons. Their early use was implicit in this view. Bearing in mind the nuclear superiority enjoyed by the USA at the time and with Britain the only West European country to possess such weapons, the short war strategy was less risky than it was to become in the age of the super power nuclear "balance of terror" and of intermediate range nuclear weapons deployed in Europe.

For Britain the philosophy was particularly convenient. It justified the continuation of the strategic nuclear deterrent capability and weakened the case for the simultaneous maintenance of substantial numbers of conventional forces and reserves neither of which the country could afford in the quantities needed to defend Europe alongside the USA against the growing Soviet threat. If the war was to be short there would be no time for reserves to be mobilised and despatched to fight nor would stockpiles of ammunition and war stores to equip them be required. The need for maritime forces to safeguard reinforcement and resupply convoys to Europe from the New World could also be questioned, for in the short war scenario the convoys would not reach Europe before the dropping of thermo-nuclear bombs had ended hostilities.

There was another advantage for Britain in this scenario. Smaller forces and few reserves meant that manpower could be released to meet the urgent needs of industry. Military national service, often considered to be an obstacle to Britain's industrial recovery, could be ended. The decision of a Conservative Government in 1957 to take this step in 1962 was one of the more important results of the Macmillan strategic policy. Adverse though the effects of this decision on the moral fibre, strength of character, and general behaviour of the country's youth may, in retrospect, appear, it has to be remembered that in the early sixties the beguiling concept of "full employment" was constantly in ministerial minds as an achievable aim; in the mid eighties with the total of registered unemployed obstinately refusing to fall below the three million mark, it is astonishing to recall that in July 1965 this total had fallen to a paltry 280,000.

Overseas Withdrawal. The Next Phase of Readjustment.

Despite Suez, Macmillan proved no less anxious than Attlee to maintain Britain's position in the world and to provide the military strength appropriate to this condition. The importance he attached to a nuclear capability has already been noted and the Nassau agreement with President Kennedy in 1962 to update this capability by the purchase of Polaris missiles from the USA and the construction of large submarines in which to carry them followed naturally from this view. This nuclear capability and the maintenance of the British Army of the Rhine and its supporting Tactical Air Force in West Germany ensured a contribution to European defence appropriate to a major power. Further afield, British influence could be wielded by continuing the almost worldwide military presence which had been rebuilt after the war, especially in the Middle East and South East Asia.

Despite the manpower reductions originated by Sandys and by the ending of National Service, the costs of the Macmillan policy continued to rise. By the early sixties the dawn of the technological advance was breaking, but the expense of the new weapons associated with this advance was daunting, and early British attempts to participate in it, such as the Blue Streak and Blue Water rockets, had to be cancelled. In 1964–65 the last defence budget of the Conservative years totalled £2,000 million, or some seven per cent of gross national product, the largest proportion of national wealth then devoted to defence, except for the USSR (twelve per cent) and the USA (nine per cent).[8] But it was the costs of the European and overseas commitments, and their adverse effects on an economy still bedevilled by balance of payments problems, that caused most concern.

By the end of the second post war decade, despite the fundamental adjustments to British defence policy resulting from the Sandys review and the end of National Service, that policy was again proving to be over-ambitious in relation to what the country could realistically afford. Corrective measures were required.

Elected in the autumn of 1964, the new Labour Government lost no time in planning them. In March 1965 Denis Healey, the new Defence Secretary, explained to the Commons the urgency of the situation:

> *"Defence costs were rising at a rate completely incompatible with our economic growth. Even so the government were failing to get value for the colossal sums of money that they were spending."*
>
> *"The fact remains that we are still spending a higher proportion of our national wealth on our defence forces than any other country of our size, than any of our main competitors in world trade, and this expenditure bears particularly heavily on our balance of payments*

and on the type of resources, both in manpower and in manufacturing capacity, which we need most of all to get our economic situation right."[9]

The main financial objective of the 1966 Defence Review was a target defence budget in 1969–70 of £2,000 million at 1964 price levels, about six per cent of estimated gross national product. The aims of the review were threefold, to bring defence expenditure into balance with the nation's resources, to reduce overstretch in the forces, and to cut the foreign exchange costs of defence. The starting point was a 1966–67 budget of £2,172 million and armed forces of 421,000 in April 1966. Of this budget total £605 million (27.8 per cent) were the directly attributable costs of forces deployed in Europe and other parts of the world.

TABLE 1.1
BRITAIN'S ARMED FORCES
Costs of Overseas Deployments 1966–67[10]

Area	*Cost £millions*
Germany (incl. Berlin)	203
Far East (excl. Hong Kong)	235
Hong Kong	16
Middle East	66
Mediterranean	67
Other areas (Simonstown, Caribbean, etc.)	18
	605

This is not the place to recall the stormy story of the 1966 Defence review.[11] Its aims, were economic, primarily to reduce the adverse effects of overseas defence costs on the country's balance of payments. But spending less on overseas defence meant reductions in military commitments, in short bringing the forces home. Like Attlee before him, Harold Wilson was at first reluctant to weaken Britain's worldwide influence in this way:

> *"Whatever we may do in the field of cost-effectiveness, value for money, and a stringent view of expenditure, we cannot afford to relinquish our world-wide role which, for short-hand purposes, is sometimes called our East of Suez role."*[12]

His Defence Secretary supported this stance with a statesmanlike and in some ways farseeing view:

> *"But the fact is – and I do ask Hon. Members to recognise this – that if we simply abdicated the responsibility we now carry, without making any arrangements to share them or to hand them over to any body, there is a grave risk that some part of this great area would dissolve into violence and chaos, for we must face the fact that the main danger of war today lies outside Europe and not inside it."*[13]

These shafts of strategic realism briefly illuminated the dull commercial canvas of the 1966 Defence Review but in the end they were extinguished by the pressure of economic events at home.

In 1966, cuts in the projected levels of defence spending were essential on economic grounds; the problem was how and where to make them. Once again – and it would not be for the last time – the Government found itself burdened with two commitments, the maintenance of which lay at the heart of British defence and strategic policy, the independent strategic nuclear deterrent force and the Brussels Treaty commitment to deploy an army and a tactical air force in West Germany. Both were deemed to be sacrosanct. In any case the Polaris programme was by then too far advanced for outright cancellation although it proved possible to abandon the fifth submarine without financial penalty. As for the forces in Germany, then costing some £89 million in valuable foreign exchange, all that could be done was to revive the arguments with the Federal Republic over offset purchases or other means of reducing this running sore in our balance of payments problem, apart from bringing home to the United Kingdom a brigade from the British Army of the Rhine and a helicopter squadron from Royal Air Force Germany (units returned to Germany at a later date).

There remained the costs of Britain's non-European overseas deployments, another heavy drain on the country's foreign exchange. But how could these costs be reduced when the Government ruled out withdrawals on strategic grounds? Healey resorted to the novel and ingenious remedy of the strategic fudge. The use of overseas forces in war would be subject to severe political limitations, no major operations except in conjunction with allies, no military assistance to another country unless that country was prepared to provide the necessary facilities, and no maintenance of defence facilities in an independent country against its wishes.

From this constricting web it was but a short step not only to propound justificatory reasons for reductions in the forces deployed overseas, but also for abandoning particular military capabilities, the need for which, it could now be argued, would be extremely unlikely in view of the limitations described above. Thus did the 1966 Defence Review set out to destroy the case for the deployment by Britain of aircraft carriers east of Suez and, by inference, for the maintenance of the aircraft carrier and naval fixed wing air component of a balanced fleet.

This proposed transformation of the Royal Navy into an offshore force, unable to operate safely outside the range of shore-based air support was, to say the least, strategically questionable. In 1966 it was the largest navy in Western Europe and, following the withdrawal of France from the NATO military structure, the only European navy in the Allied Command Atlantic with a carrier borne air component. The expansion of the Soviet navy into an ocean-going force capable of distant deployments had already begun, especially in the Mediterranean. But the British Government chose to ignore the broad strategic implications of its economically inspired defence review of 1966. In any case, it was anxious to extend the "short war" philosophy to include naval forces and in the 1967 Defence White Paper pointed out that:

> *"It is no longer realistic for the Alliance to attempt to provide maritime forces for conducting a prolonged war at sea after a strategic nuclear exchange. Deterrence must be the first purpose of NATO's naval forces too."* [14]

Throughout 1967 the economic situation of Britain continued to worsen and the deficit on the balance of payments to grow. In a final effort to arrest this decline sterling was devalued from $2.67 to $2.40 on 18th November and the Chancellor of the Exchequer, James Callaghan, resigned. On January 16 1968 the Prime Minister announced in the Commons that the Government had carried out a detailed and searching review of the whole range of public expenditure as one of the measures necessary for a radical solution of the country's balance of payments problems.

Wilson went on to announce yet more cuts in future levels of defence spending in addition to those already introduced during the past two years. It was clear that the defence budget would be the worst sufferer in the programme of national retrenchment, and reductions in overseas defence expenditure the principal weapon in the fight to restore the balance of payments. In justification, the Government introduced into the argument an important principle embracing the relationship between the nation's economic and military strength:

> *"It is not only in our own interests but in those of our friends and allies for this country to strengthen its economic base quickly and decisively. There is no military strength whether for Britain or for our alliances except on the basis of economic strength; and it is on this basis that we best ensure the security of this country."* [15]

As a principle for sound and responsible government this argument is impeccable. Yet from 1964, Labour administrations have consistently awarded priority in the allocation of the country's financial resources (i.e. the fruits of its economic strength) to the maintenance and enlargement of the whole fabric of the Welfare State with defence occupying a lower place in the financial pecking order. This was the thrust of Wilson's economic policy throughout the six years of his Government.

By 1970 the economy was in better shape and the balance of payments actually in surplus as a result of the devaluation of sterling and the subsequent measures of the new Chancellor, Roy Jenkins. But no effort was made to halt the planned reductions in forces manpower or to re-examine the economic necessity for the abandonment of so many overseas military commitments. So it was that economic pressures forced Wilson and Healey to complete a strategic somersault from the bragadoccio of 1964 that "we cannot afford to relinquish our world role" to the almost total abandonment of that role and to a policy whereby:

> *"Britain's defence effort will in future be concentrated mainly in Europe and in the North Atlantic area."* [16]

Altogether, it was a major shift of policy which took no less than four Defence White Papers to explain during 1967–68. The economic constraints facing the Government in 1964 were the main reason for the substantial reductions in Britain's military strength and in her overseas defence commitments. These were the outward and visible signs of the final transformation of Britain from a Great Power – one of the "post war 'Big Three' " – to a middle rank European nation and they laid the foundations for a defence and strategic policy which has endured to this day, namely, the maintenance of an independent strategic nuclear deterrent force and of a major conventional contribution of land, sea and air forces to the Alliance for the defence of the NATO area.

However, in its eagerness to hasten the introduction of the cuts and to accelerate the withdrawal programme once it had been agreed, the Government failed to examine one important aspect of the fundamental switch in British defence and strategic policy which it was determined to bring about.

In none of Healey's cascade of defence statements was there to be found any reference to the needs of national security – the defence of the realm, for example – as opposed to those of Alliance security and the British contribution to it. Throughout, national interests were assumed to be satisfactorily dealt with by the NATO strategic plan for the defence of Western Europe and by the assignment of British forces to NATO commands to participate in that plan. The foundation of Britain's security was judged to lie in the maintenance of peace in Europe, almost regardless of what went on in the world outside.

But the withdrawal into Europe and the substantial reductions in the size of the British armed forces which this concentration would bring about meant that a far higher proportion of those forces would now be assigned to NATO than had been the case previously. Virtually the whole of the Royal Navy's operational fleet would now be normally deployed in European waters; more importantly, over thirty per cent of the standing army would be required to maintain the Brussels Treaty commitment of 55,000 men in Rhine Army as opposed to some fourteen per cent in the mid-fifties, together with ten per cent of the Royal Air Force compared with four per cent before. Would the needs of national security best be served by this subordination of so much of the country's military capability to NATO plans? Indeed, was the composition of the multi-role contribution to the defence of Europe the most appropriate for Britain to make, bearing in mind her unique geo-strategic position in Western Europe, her tradition of maritime strength and expertise, and the changing nature of the military threats to the NATO area and to areas of strategic importance to the West beyond it?

Neither in 1966, 1975, nor 1981 were these questions examined. By 1986 this continuous relegation of an admittedly thorny political problem to the "Too Difficult" tray of successive foreign and defence ministers had resulted in an unacceptable imbalance in the shape and size of Britain's armed forces still structured to meet the needs of an increasingly obsolete NATO strategy.

The economic strength which, so it was claimed, is the foundation on which military strength can be sustained, depends for its achievement on the successful management of the national economy as a whole. A favourable balance of payments is one aspect of such management, the most efficient and productive employment of the nation's manpower is another, although less important in the mid-eighties than it was in the mid-sixties.

In the past, Labour had consistently claimed that the allocation of substantial numbers of the working population to the armed forces was a hindrance to the achievement of higher levels of production in manufacturing industry and hence to the increase in exports which was such a vital necessity. But once in office, these claims were put aside.

The vast extension of the Welfare State which took pride of place in the Government's priorities could not be carried out without an enormous increase in the number of people required to administer it. In the five years 1964–69 armed forces manpower was reduced by 9.5 per cent from 423,100 to 382,900. But in 1966 alone the number of people employed in government departments soared by over 24,000 bringing the strength of the civil service up to a record 457,563. Under Labour, Britain was fast becoming over administered and under defended.

The Heath Interlude

Throughout its brief tenure of office the Conservative government of 1970–74 accepted the broad pattern of allocations within the defence budget which had emerged from the tumultuous Healey years, continued to spend more on social security and education than on defence, and proved just as dilatory as Labour over the ordering of new weapons and equipment.

However, whilst not disputing the general thrust of a strategic policy which gave priority to the defence of the NATO area, Heath and his Foreign Secretary, Sir Alec Douglas-Home (now Lord Home of the Hirsel) recognised that there were more far-flung threats to British and Alliance interests. The five-power arrangements for the defence of Malaysia and Singapore, embodied in the formation of the ANZUK force with its substantial British component, was the sole example of a British government initiating a regional defence pact with local nations to replace the British military presence which Labour's policy of complete military withdrawal from east of Suez sought to end.

The attempt to sell limited categories of arms to South Africa was part of this more widespread strategic pattern as was the decision announced in the 1970 supplementary Statement on Defence Policy to retain the aircraft carrier, HMS *Ark Royal*, in active commission until the late 1970s. This continued the Royal Navy's ability to deploy, wherever it was needed, a strong surface task force with its own integral air support.

One of the objectives of the Heath government's defence policy was:

> *"to establish and maintain a sound financial basis on which to develop and carry out defence policy and plans in the years ahead"*.[17]

But the dramatic events of the autumn of 1973, culminating in OPEC's release of its oil price weapon, which was to cause such enormous damage to the vulnerable economies of Western Europe, especially to that of Britain, quickly put paid to this desirable aim, the achievement of which has so often eluded the efforts of British governments in the post-war years. In December of that year, the Chancellor of the Exchequer, Anthony Barber (now Lord Barber) was obliged to cut £178 million from the planned 1974–75 defence estimates of £3,365 million. With another stroke of the salami-slicer £162 million was removed from the weapons and equipment programme, and £16 million from the capital works budget. Even before the unexpected general election in February 1974, it was clear that the rise in inflation induced by the OPEC action would render inevitable a substantial reduction in government spending in Britain and that the defence budget was bound to suffer.

1974–79. The Lean Years

Throughout the Heath years, the Tribune group of the Parliamentary Labour Party and its allies in the Trades Union Congress had conducted a vociferous campaign aimed at Britain's level of defence expenditure. In February 1974 they were rewarded by the Labour Party's manifesto pledge to "*progressively reduce the burden of Britain's defence spending to bring our costs into line with those carried by our main European allies*".[18] The proportion of Gross National Product spent on defence in the other countries of NATO Europe was certainly a convenient means of claiming to a gullible and relatively uninterested electorate that Britain was contributing more than she could afford to Alliance security. In 1974 she was still top of this particular statistical league table except for Portugal. But the gross national products of both France and West Germany were far larger in money terms than that of Britain and as a result these two "main European allies" were actually spending more on defence than Britain, in the case of West Germany considerably more.

In February 1974 the second Wilson administration inherited a reduced defence budget for 1974–75 of £3,187 million (approx 5.7 per cent of GNP) and 349,300 United Kingdom personnel in the armed forces compared with its own last defence budget in 1969–70 of £2,266 million and 383,000 men and women serving their country. At once the new government had to deal with the most serious economic consequence of the rise in the oil price, a

TABLE 1.2
The Western Alliance. Defence Expenditures 1976–86

COUNTRY	1975 GDP ($US billion)	Def. Exp. 1976 ($US billion)	1976 % of GDP spent on defence	Per capita Def. Exp. 1976 ($US)	1985 GDP ($US billion)	1986 Def. Exp. ($US billion)	1986 % of 1985 GDP on defence	Per capita Def. Exp. 1986 ($US)
USA	1,498.8	100.1	6.67	460	3,839.0	266.6	6.9	1,115
NATO Europe German Federal Republic	441.6	12.60	2.85	255	621.74	19.77	3.3	324
France	359.2	10.66	2.96	261	511.44	20.13	4.0	365
Britain	226.0	10.35	4.5	209	400.10	22.62	5.2	401
Italy	177.5	3.47	1.95	77	360.64	0.3	2.7	162
Spain	94.5	2.15	2.27	9	169.14	3.6	2.1	97
Pacific Japan	502.5	5.058	1.0	45	1,996.7	21.36	1.07	109
USSR						295.0 (est)	12–17 (est)	

Source: "The Military Balance" 1975–76 and 1986–87 (IISS London)

substantial increase in the rate of domestic inflation. In Britain the Retail Price Index (RPI) rose from an annual rate of 8.9 per cent in 1972–73 to one of 20 per cent in 1974–75. The costs of new weapons and equipment began to rise at an even faster rate than domestic inflation. No government, but particularly no Labour administration determined to maintain welfare spending and hamstrung by its manifesto commitment, could responsibly raise the level of defence spending by the amounts that would be needed to hold its real value. Inevitably, there was a substantial fall in real terms in British defence spending between 1974 and 1979.

There was no way of avoiding another defence review. Its findings were published in the 1975 Statement on the Defence Estimates and represented "*the results of a rigorous and fundamental analysis of every aspect of Britain's defence commitments and capabilities*". Once again, as in its last review almost ten years before, the government claimed that in the light of this analysis changes were necessary in order to reduce the burden of defence expenditure on the national economy and release resources for investment and the balance of payments. Moreover in the broader international context:

> "*The Government recognised, from the moment they took office, the need to tailor our defence commitments and capabilities to our economic and political position as a middle-rank European power, and to ensure a modern and effective defence system geared to what we can afford. This cannot be done by relaxation of vigilance, wishful thinking, and blindness to political and economic trends.*"[19]

The review resulted in estimated savings at 1974 prices of £4,700 million over the years to 1983–84 in future defence spending and of nearly £1,500 million to 1978–79. Over ten years it would reduce the proportion of GNP spent on defence from 5.5 per cent to 4.5 per cent. In the five years from April 1974 manpower reductions would be of the order of 38,000 (11 per cent) for the armed forces and 30,000 (10 per cent) for their civilian support, with the largest reductions in the strength of the Royal Air Force and in the total of locally-employed civilians overseas. The numbers of UK civilians would fall by only 6 per cent, reflecting the influence of the Trade Unions particularly evident in the decision to retain all four Royal Dockyards in the United Kingdom despite the cuts in fleet strength which were planned and their record of low productivity. In the event, by April 1979 these manpower targets had been broadly achieved with 315,000 United Kingdom personnel in the armed forces against a target of 311,300 and 262,900 Ministry of Defence civilians (target 265,600).

Using the Review's decision to withdraw British naval forces from Singapore, the West Indies and the Mediterranean in justification, the Government would effect "*progressive reductions of one-seventh in planned numbers of destroyers, frigates and mine countermeasures vessels with consequential reductions in afloat support*".[20] The size of the Army would be adjusted to meet the new framework of defence priorities and the demands of the economy, mainly by eliminating the brigade level of command, and improving the man-to-weapon ratio. In the Royal Air Force there would be a substantial reduction in the transport fleet and a smaller cut in the numbers of maritime patrol aircraft, but the numbers of front-line combat aircraft committed to NATO would be maintained.

Although the review was muted in its references to cuts in equipment and weapon programmes, it was clear that some curtailment of these programmes would be inevitable. Obliged, after the completion of the review, to accept the Treasury's demands for a further cut of £110 million at 1974 survey prices in the 1976–77 budget, Roy Mason, the Defence Secretary, admitted that "*it will mean that equipment purchases will have to be adjusted, works and building programmes deferred and some further job opportunities lost*"[21]. Nevertheless the extent of the cuts in the country's defence capabilities was less than that demanded by the Tribune Group and its TUC allies in their more irresponsible moments and for this Mason and his successor, Frederick Mulley (now Lord Mulley), must be given credit.

Throughout the Government's tenure of office they successfully strove to limit the damage to national security which submission to the demands of their left-wing colleagues would have caused.

In particular, the ordering of twenty-five Sea Harrier VSTOL aircraft for the Royal Navy in May 1975 and the continuation of the "Through Deck Cruiser" building programme (the *Invincible* class of small aircraft carriers) reversed Healey's much criticised decision of 1966 to do away with fixed wing naval aviation. Without this reversal of policy, the Falklands campaign could not have been comtemplated, let alone undertaken, seven years later.

Of course, in 1975 there was no strategic justification for these major reductions in Britain's armed forces and, paradoxically, the Defence Review admitted as much. After describing the cuts to be made it went on to explain how the military balance in Europe between NATO and the Warsaw Pact was deteriorating to the disadvantage of NATO. In the maritime sphere, the inconsistency of a policy which, for reasons of economy, would substantially reduce NATO's "mainly British" naval forces in the Eastern Atlantic in the face of the emergence of the Soviet Union as a maritime super-power, was particularly marked.

The British Government decided on the areas in which the country's contribution to the Alliance should be concentrated as a result of the review. Its prior consultations with NATO amounted to presenting it with a "fait accompli" and only minor adjustments to the reductions were made in response to the comments of Brussels. No attempt was made, as none had been made in 1966, to ask the Allies for their views on the most significant contribution Britain could make in her straitened economic circumstances, specifically whether yet another reduction in her maritime forces was to be preferred to cuts in other areas such as land or air forces assigned to the

European command. Was it surprising that when presented with the British proposals:

> *"Our allies were disquieted by the scale of the reductions we proposed and the weakening effect they would have on NATO's conventional capability vis-a-vis the Warsaw Pact if they were not offset by compensatory measures"?*[22]

The 1969 Defence Statement had set out the foundations of Britain's defence and strategic policy in her new role as a middle-rank European power following her military withdrawal from east of Suez. The policy of the four Cs, as it may be described remains in force today.

Concentration	In Europe
Compatibility	A defence effort which the country can afford,
Contribution	To the collective security of the Alliance and inter alia to national security through the
Commitment	Of British sea, land, and air forces to the NATO military command structure for the defence of the NATO area. A similar commitment of the strategic nuclear deterrent force.

The 1975 Review elaborated on this theme by explaining in detail the areas where the Government had decided to concentrate the British defence effort in order to make the most significant contribution to "*her security and that of the Alliance*".[23] In the order listed in the Statement, these were:

> *The Central Region, the Eastern Atlantic and Channel Areas, the security of the United Kingdom and its immediate approaches, and the NATO nuclear deterrent (tactical and strategic weapons).*

In addition some specialist reinforcement capability would also be maintained.

By 1986 the short-war philosophy had been strengthened by the inexorable rise in the costs of new conventional weapons and equipment and by the impossibility of finding financial resources to produce them in sufficient quantities to maintain the country's conventional capabilities and so raise the nuclear threshold in Europe. It was not surprising that the 1986 Defence Statement listed Britain's contribution in the order:

> *"Nuclear forces, Defence of the United Kingdom, European Mainland, and Maritime forces."*[24]

For a year after the publication of the 1975 Defence Review the country's economic situation continued to deteriorate; it needed the intervention of the International Monetary Fund (IMF) and the constraints on the Government's economic policy which the IMF imposed in the autumn of 1976 to halt the decline. The further cuts of £300 million in future defence spending announced in December 1976, as part of the corrective measures, proved to be the last of the several reductions in this area of government spending to be made during the Wilson/Callaghan years.

In the spring of 1979, in a volte-face which mirrored its concern over the disastrous effects on the armed forces which the successive cuts since 1975 were by then beginning to bring about, the Government produced its last defence budget of £8.56 billion for 1979–80 and announced pay rises for the forces averaging 24.2 per cent in order to restore "comparability" by April 1980. This total, it was claimed, represented an increase over that of the previous year of 3 per cent in real terms to conform to the 1977 NATO agreement to increase defence spending by this amount annually until 1985. For Britain the nadir of the OPEC induced disarmament had been passed.

The consequences of the savage treatment meted out to Britain's defence spending from 1974 to 1979 will linger on for many years, particularly in the provision of modern equipment and weapons. For salami-slicing was endemic to the whole philosophy underlying the implementation of the succession of cuts. As a result, the ordering of medium-lift helicopters for Army support was postponed, the introduction of new anti-tank and air defence weapons for the Army was delayed, the production rate of the new Tornado aircraft reduced, and a squadron of Jaguar offensive support aircraft cancelled. Production of spare parts and ammunition was likewise reduced. Not surprisingly, as awareness of the Government's lack of interest in defence matters grew, recruitment fell back and the numbers seeking premature voluntary release rose.

Labour's policy of placing such heavy emphasis on reductions in future defence spending in its desperate search for economies, whilst failing to consider the effects of these cuts on the national economy as a whole, let alone on the strategic policy which the unfolding of world events appeared to require, was widely criticised. Discussing the adverse comments of the Commons Defence and External Affairs Sub Committee in February 1976, *The Times* pointed out that:

> *"Although the review had resulted in the loss of some 51,000 jobs, service and civilian, together with 140,000 employment opportunities forfeited in the defence industries, there was no guarantee that alternative work will be found in the right places to take up this slack . . . To cut defence spending in order to help the national economy is a rational motive, whether or not one agrees that it should prevail over other considerations. It is much less rational to make cuts just for the sake of doing so. Defence cuts have too often been viewed in isolation and not in the context of the national economy."*[25]

Ten years later Margaret Thatcher's Government also showed every sign of an excessively departmentalised approach to the abiding problem of defence cuts.

1979–86. The Conservative Record

The first Thatcher administration inherited a defence budget for 1979–80 of £8.56 billion (approx. 4.75 per cent of GDP), and armed forces of

315,000. This was the smallest total since 1945 and it included a serious shortage of trained personnel. One of the first acts of the new Government was to award substantial pay increases to the Forces to restore in full the comparability of their remuneration with that of their civilian counterparts. The election manifesto had promised to make good the worst of the deficiencies which four years of almost continuous cutbacks had caused. For the first time in over a quarter of a century, a new government came to power in Britain pledged to increase rather than to reduce spending on defence.

With this auspicious start no financial difficulties were foreseen in maintaining unimpaired the strategic policy of the 4 Cs which the Government had inherited. In July 1980, supported by a favourable vote in the House of Commons in January of that year on the question of Britain continuing to maintain an independent strategic nuclear deterrent force, Francis Pym, the Defence Secretary, announced the Government's decision to buy from the United States the Trident submarine launched ballistic missile system to replace the ageing Polaris force in this role. The original cost estimates for Trident were for up to £5 billion over fifteen years with seventy per cent being spent in Britain.

Meanwhile, however, the second cycle of Middle East oil price rises, which had begun almost as soon as the Conservatives were returned to power, and the rise in inflation which it caused, had initiated a significant recession in the economies of the western industrialised nations. In Britain the inflation rate had risen from 9.3 per cent in 1978 to no less than 18.4 per cent by the end of 1979 and, although it moderated in the following year to 13.0 per cent, further damage to the costs of new weapons and equipment and of forces' pay and pensions had been suffered. Furthermore, in the case of Trident the decision to end exchange controls in October 1979 meant that estimates of its final cost would vary dramatically in line with the marked fluctuations of the sterling-dollar exchange rate which in September 1980 had risen to the high level of $2.36 to £1.

To begin with the Ministry of Defence believed that these adverse economic developments could be taken in its stride without serious damage to the defence budget. In retrospect this is the only logical explanation for what was to prove an astonishingly over-optimistic forecast delivered to the Commons in July 1980:

> *"We intend to accommodate this (Trident costs) within the defence budget in the normal way, alongside our other major force improvements. We remain determined to uphold and, where necessary, strengthen our all-round defence capability, and that applies to our conventional forces no less than to our nuclear forces."*[26]

Just six months later, this nonchalance was shattered. Despite a temporary moratorium on equipment procurement, the defence budget showed signs of spiralling out of control under the combined effects of high inflation, unexpectedly high rates of increase in real defence costs (the Relative Price

Effect), increases in fuel costs, and the burden of the substantial pay increases awarded in 1979. Margaret Thatcher decided to appoint a minister with business experience to restore the situation and to obtain better value for money out of the defence budget, John Nott. His approach to this problem was realistic, unsentimental and directed towards financial orthodoxy.

It was soon clear to him that, even in the context of the annual real increases in defence spending to 1985–86 which the Government had pledged, cuts in programmes would have to be made and probably in other areas as well. A "review" would be needed.

"The Way Forward"[27] was a "Defence Review" by any other name.

A Conservative Government, commendably determined to maintain the undertaking given to NATO to increase defence spending by 3 per cent per annum in real terms, was understandably chary of drawing upon itself the odium of being as ill-disposed towards defence as its predecessor, but, in practice, there was little to choose between the 1975 and 1981 reviews as far as their effects on Britain's military capabilities were concerned. Once again these would be reduced.

As has been seen, the strains on the economy caused by the recession brought about by the oil price rises of 1979–80 were the cause of the 1981 review. As Nott explained:

> *"The House knows of our basic problems, which are not unique to Britain. We have a defence programme which is unbalanced and over-extended. Last year, we suffered from severe cash problems, and similar difficulties are already emerging in the current year. We cannot go on like this."*[28]

It was the banker's approach; the company chairman preparing the shareholders at the Annual General Meeting for news of a cut in the dividend.

Once again there was no prior discussion with the NATO Allies over the effects of the cuts in capabilities on the British conventional contribution to NATO, nor was the opportunity taken to initiate a strategic discussion within NATO on what might now be the most useful and effective contribution given the country's economic state and the inevitable necessity for the scope of the multi-role contribution to be reduced in one way or another.

For reduced it would have to be and after their experience with previous reviews of British defence policy, it can have come as no surprise to the NATO Allies to hear that the Royal Navy would suffer the largest manpower cuts of the three services, that its surface fleet would be again reduced and that, in consequence, Britain's contribution to NATO's maritime forces in the Eastern Atlantic would be cut by about 15 per cent. As in 1966 over the future of the aircraft carrier force, so in 1981 there were introduced into the Review new concepts, this time for the conduct of anti-submarine warfare, the validity of which could be strongly questioned on technical and operational grounds. These were used to provide justification for the reductions in the country's naval forces that were proposed.

Yet in two important respects the Nott review displayed a novel realism and a welcome awareness of the changing nature of the military threats both to the NATO area in general and to Britain in particular which improved and enlarged Soviet capabilities were bringing about. For the first time in post war history the defence of the United Kingdom itself was examined, "*especially in its role as a crucial reinforcement base for NATO*" – and some long overdue improvements set in train, notably in air defence and in the expansion and re-equipment of the reserve forces. Further afield, despite the ritual incantation that "*the forward defence of Germany is the forward defence of the United Kingdom itself*", it was admitted that:

> "*In reviewing our defence programme the Government have had to look far beyond the confines of our small corner of Europe. We must recognise the threat to our peace and prosperity from the other side of the globe.*"[29]

For this reason measures to provide Britain with an "out of area" capability would be maintained and in some cases improved. It was ironical that less than a year later the Government did indeed have to look far beyond the confines of Europe and in a totally unexpected direction to re-possess a remote piece of British real estate, a task which could only be performed by maritime forces such as those the necessity for which both Healey and Nott had been at pains to question.

The changes in resource allocation resulting from these small signs of realism in British strategic thought were only marginal. The object of the 1981 Review was in effect to reduce the size of the conventional forces and adjust their stocks of new weapons and equipment to levels which could be afforded, as far as could be foreseen, during the incidence of the highest costs of the Trident programme from 1985–95. But the areas in which reductions and adjustments could be made were limited by political considerations and by commitment to a major collaborative procurement programme with European allies.

Locked, as it was at the time of the review, in one of its recurring battles with Brussels over the scale of the British contribution to EEC budget, the Foreign Office opposed any tampering with the strategic status quo in Europe in which the deployment of US, British and French forces in the Federal Republic was a pivotal factor. "*The Way Forward*" confirmed that:

> "*Despite the financial pressures on our defence effort, the Government has decided that this contribution (the Brussels Treaty commitment to maintain 55,000 troops and a tactical air force in West Germany) is so important to the Alliance's military posture and its political cohesion that it must be maintained.*"[30]

By 1981, fifty-three Tornado GR1 strike/attack aircraft and eighteen Tornado ADV interceptors had been ordered and the programme to procure 220 GR1s and 165 ADVs over a period of ten years was too far advanced to permit any reduction. But Nott was aware that the total cost of the programme, calculated on the same basis as that for Trident, would be at least as heavy.[1] Given the parameters within which the 1981 Review had to be prepared, the thrust of its conclusions was almost inevitable.

The Trident Factor

Since 1980 successive defence secretaries have continued to uphold the Pym pledge that the costs of Trident could be accommodated within the defence budget without detriment to the major re-equipment programmes of the conventional forces or to their ability to meet their commitments and continue the multi-role contribution to NATO. But the increasing doubts as to whether this pledge can be fulfilled have been augmented by the Government's decision to end its commitment to an annual growth in the defence budget of three per cent in real terms from 1985–86 and to announce future defence spending plans to 1988–89 which will amount to a reduction of six per cent in real terms over the three year period.[31] This is just the period when Trident costs will be rising towards their zenith.

By 1986 the Trident programme was on schedule and the first of the four submarines (SSBN 05) had been ordered from Vickers Shipbuilders and Engineers at Barrow. The latest estimate of the total cost was £9.265 billion at average 1986/87 prices using a sterling/dollar exchange rate of $1.50 to £1 and broken down in percentage terms as follows:[32]

	Per cent
Submarines (less weapons system equipment)	29
Weapons System Equipment	23
Missiles	13
Shore Construction	7
Warhead, Miscellaneous, unallocated contingency, etc	28
	100

By the end of 1986, almost £1.00 billion had been spent and a further £2.00 billion contractually committed. By 1988–89 the annual costs will be around £900 million. During the peak years, the programme may sustain employment for up to 15,000 annually in industries directly concerned with the programme and another 12,000 indirectly in supporting industries.

The Government's answer to those who doubt the validity of Pym pledge is that Trident expenditure has to be seen in context. For example, over the twenty-year period of the programme the cost of £9.265 billion compares with expenditure on British forces in Germany over a comparable period

1 In 1980, the unit cost of one Tornado GR1 aircraft was nine million pounds; by 1986 this had risen to seventeen million.

at current levels of £46billion, or nearly five times as much.[33] But such arguments are unconvincing. The conventional equipment budgets of all three services are bound to suffer during the peak years at least of the Trident programme and because for budgetary purposes it is a sea-based system it will be the Royal Navy's equipment programme that will suffer most. Indeed, the delays in the ordering of Type 23 frigates show that this is already happening. Adherence to the 'short war' philosophy with the accompanying questioning of the need for surface warships is not the sole reason for the relatively severe treatment already accorded by successive administrations to the Royal Navy compared with that meted out to the other two Services.

Strategically, the effect of introducing Trident at the expense of conventional capabilities is to give priority to a deterrent system based on nuclear weapons, and to lower the nuclear threshold in Europe.

> *"It is claimed that if we have Trident we shall have to cut back on conventional weapons, but that, I suggest, misses the key point. The central question is not whether if we have Trident we shall have less to spend on conventional weapons – that is obviously the case – but whether the sum of money to be spent on Trident will be a better addition to Britain's and NATO's defences than the same sum of money spent on conventional weapons. That is the key question, and as my Right Hon. Friend the Prime Minister recently stated in the House, our view is that the sum being spent on Trident will give us an amount of deterrence which we could not possibly get by spending the same sum on conventional weapons."*[34]

Nevertheless, the Trident programme deserves to be supported. Even so, with equipment and weapon costs at their present levels no British government, however favourably disposed towards expenditure on national security can afford to finance the exceptional capital costs of modernising its strategic nuclear deterrent force within the limits of its planned annual defence budget without seriously weakening the conventional arms.

Since this type of force only requires a new weapons and delivery system about once every quarter of a century, the costs of a modernisation programme should be financed annually over the life of the programme by a supplementary estimate separate from and in addition to the budget for the conventional forces and financed directly by the Treasury, as were the costs of the Falklands campaign. There should be an annual parliamentary debate on this estimate during which the government could report on the progress of the programme.

As yet there are no signs of the Government adopting such a procedure. But without it David Greenwood's gloomy forecast of the effects of attempting to finance Trident by adjustments to other programmes may well prove to have been justified.[35]

British Forces in Germany. An Economic Absurdity

It was unfortunate that a minister attempting to put the costs of the Trident programme over its twenty-year life in the context of other expensive commitments over a similar period should have used British Forces in Germany for his comparison (see page 21).

By 1986, the contrast between the economic state of health of Britain and West Germany had transformed this deployment into an act of generous philanthropy by the United Kingdom which was much more in Britain's political than national military interests to provide. Nor was it genuinely of overall assistance to NATO because of the imbalance in Britain's capabilities which its maintenance was causing.

The economy of West Germany is far stronger than that of any other NATO European nation and, along with the United States dollar and the Japanese yen, the deutschmark rates as one of the "Big Three" in the world's foreign exchange markets. In the Davos Symposium's 1986 survey of international competitiveness West Germany occupied fourth place, Britain fifteenth. West Germany's trade suplus contrasts starkly with the huge deficit in the United States and the strength of the deutschmark against the dollar in 1986 reflected this relationship. In 1985 West Germany's Gross Domestic Product at $621.74 billion was the highest in the western world except for the United States and Japan. Britain's was $480.60 billion. Yet in the same year, as determined by all the internationally accepted measurements of a nation's defence effort (total defence expenditure, its percentage of GDP, and per capita expenditure), West Germany was spending less than Britain.[36]

In 1986–87 Britain spent £3.4 billion (nineteen per cent of its defence budget) on the directly attributable costs of maintaining thirty-four per cent of its standing army and eleven per cent of its air force in West Germany to defend 65 kilometres of the inner German frontier. This sum included an annual outflow of the equivalent of £966 million in deutschmarks, much of it going to provide employment for the 22,600 German civilians required to provide the domestic needs of the British garrisons. This was by far the largest item in the defence balance of payments which was in deficit to the tune of £1.3 billion as a result.[37]

The figures speak for themselves. This situation reveals how little the ideas of equitable burden-sharing of the costs of defending the NATO area and of military role specialisation amongst the allies have made progress. More seriously, it has become a matter for concern that so much of the British defence effort should be expended on maintaining an outdated strategic scenario with a contribution which prejudices national defence needs and which is no longer the most appropriate and cost-effective for Britain to make.

Management Reforms and the Search for Cost-Effectiveness

Nott's successor, Michael Heseltine, introduced a number of reforms in a wide-ranging search for efficiency and cost-effectiveness in the management of Britain's defence effort. His most important initiative was to restructure completely the country's higher organisation for Defence in order to obtain the best possible value in defence output from the very substantial resources which the Government was prepared to commit to national security. (The 1984–85 defence budget of £17.03 billion represented no less than 5.4 per cent of Gross Domestic Product.) From his initial examination of its structure Heseltine had concluded with with some justification that the Ministry of Defence – then responsible for some 320,000 uniformed personnel and 230,000 civilian staff, of which almost 20,000 were employed in the Ministry itself – was less economical and efficient than it should be. Included in the new management structure was the establishment of a new Office of Management and Budget (OMB) under the Second Permanent Under Secretary of the Ministry. This would provide stronger budgetary control of the defence programme and of resource allocation and priorities.

Stronger control is certainly needed. Year after year, the Ministry is taken to task either by the Comptroller and Auditor General or by the Commons Select Committee on Defence for shortcomings in its financial control procedures. To take but one example, in August 1986 the former Comptroller reported that the Defence Ministry had overspent by £938 million on twelve major defence contracts and had paid out over £200 million on a further seven projects which were later concelled. (See Chapter 6.) For a government which in seven years had succeeded in raising the propotion of the defence budget spent on equipment from 39.7 per cent to 44.6 per cent with manpower costs cut from 42.6 per cent to 36.4 per cent. the revelation of these shortcomings must have been especially frustrating.

Economic Efficiency. Achievements and Limitations

Introducing the 1986–87 defence estimates to the Commons, George Younger – who had succeeded Heseltine after the latter's abrupt resignation in January 1986 – justifiably claimed substantial achievements on the part of the Government in its management of defence policy. The level of the defence budget is now about 20 per cent higher in real terms than it was in 1979. With an equipment budget of 45 per cent of the whole, Britain, he claimed, was now spending a higher proportion on equipment than any other NATO country. The introduction of competitive tendering for new equipment contracts was leading to major savings. Within the forces the "teeth to tail" ratios had been improved and there had been a reduction of 77,000 (30 per cent) in the numbers of civil servants employed to support them. Privatisation of services was being introduced wherever this might lead to improvements in efficiency and economies in costs. Forces pay and conditions had been transformed "*to reflect the esteem in which they are held by this Government and by society as a whole.*"[38]

Nevertheless, the doubts remain. Will the Pym pledge he upheld throughout the life of the Trident programme? By 1986 it was already becoming part-worn at the edges. To the extent of the severe cuts in naval manpower and in the size of the fleet, the maritime defence capabilities of the country had been neither upheld nor strengthened. In the 1986 defence debate in the Commons, Younger admitted that:

> *"There is no question of having to withdraw from any of our major commitments or any major part of them . . . we are having to take difficult decisions about order dates."*[39]

It was not only in equipment programmes that problems were beginning to appear. Necessary though the administrative slimming diet prescribed by Heseltine undoubtedly was, signs of "overstretch" were becoming evident, particularly in the Royal Navy where ship programmes had to be adjusted to allow more time at base ports. Shortages of officers were causing concern, particularly of RAF pilots, whilst redundant merchant navy officers were being recruited into the Royal Navy to meet a shortfall of trained watch-keeping and warfare officers. There were slight but worrying increases in the rates of voluntary outflow of officers and of premature voluntary release by servicemen. It was clear that the barrel of cost-effective and economy-creating savings had been scraped clean.

For forces manpower policy the implications of the Conservative ceiling on future defence spending are serious. In 1979 the Government inherited a total of 315,000 United Kingdom personnel serving in the Armed Forces. Nott's economic advisers correctly foresaw that the optimistic increase to 333,800 by April 1981 could not be maintained even during a period of sustained growth in the defence budget. If they had been implemented in full, the reductions in manpower proposed in "The Way Forward" would have cut the total back to 316,000, a mere one thousand more than Labour's 1979 bequest. As it is, the next general election will be fought with total armed forces of around 320,000 if held in 1988, or 321,000 if a year earlier. Clearly, "*We cannot go on like this*." Either commitments will have to be cut or new sources of less expensive manpower tapped. The policy of high cost, all-regular, long-service professional armed forces is breaking down.

In the run up to the general election the Government has deliberately abandoned its policy of modest real growth in defence spending in favour of much higher growth in social programmes, largely necessitated by the continuing high level of unemployment. Its public expenditure plans show that by 1988–89 spending on social security (£45.9 billion) and on health and personal social services (£19.1 billion) will have overtaken that on defence (£19.0 billion). During this period the defence budget will grow by only 4 per cent compared with increases three to four times as great in those for employment, health, social security and the Home Office (law and order). Once again, Welfare will have triumphed over Weapons in its share of national resources. A new government, whatever its political complexion, must address itself with some urgency to the problem of imaginative new defence policies both in manpower and in procurement whereby the requirements of national security and the need to reduce unemployment can be constructively combined.

Meanwhile, this sombre review of the economic limitations which constrict Britain's defence spending is best completed by summarising the conclusions which the all-party House of Commons Defence Committee drew from its examination of the defence budgets planned from 1986–87 to 1988–89.[40]

> *"Following the ending of the commitment to annual growth of 3 per cent in real terms, there will, instead of the broadly level funding expected in 1985, be a planned reduction of more than 4½ per cent in real terms over the next three years;"*
> *"That other factors may increase this figure to some 7 per cent;"*
> *"That management of the budget and improved efficiency alone will not avoid consequent cuts or delays particularly on equipment;"*
> *"That there is a risk of an adverse effect on operational capability, but not in itself amounting to the ending of a major role or commitment;"*
> *"That any further economies will have a direct effect on capability;'*
> *"And that the Ministry of Defence has moved from the apparent complacency which so exasperated us last year to a more realistic approach, which involves taking decisions long overdue."*
> *"Finally, we note that this reduction in defence expenditure comes at a time when, in the view of the Secretary of State, the threat to our security is no less than it was, and in some respects greater."*

This could have been written just as well in 1966, 1975, or 1981. When will it be written again? Is it in Britain's interest that it should have to be written again? For now there are no barrels left to scrape.

Footnote on the Future

Compared with the record of Labour in the sixties and seventies the Conservative management of the British economy since 1979 has been more successful. Nevertheless the overall financial situation remains fragile with the inherent weaknesses of the economy constantly exposing it to the effects of international developments beyond the ability of any British government to control. The price of oil, for example, is a major determinant of sterling's relationship with the other currencies of the OECD nations, and the impact of the sterling dollar rate on the costs of the Trident programme has already been mentioned (page 18). Although helpful, the effects of the lower oil prices experienced during 1986 will not be as lastingly beneficial to the British defence budget as the rises of the previous decade were damaging, for by the spring of 1987 the oil price was heading upwards once more.

So is the cycle of occasional feast and much more frequent famine that has characterised the pattern of British defence spending for the past twenty years likely to continue after the next general election? All the signs point to an affirmative answer whatever the election result. By the spring of 1986, the six year feast with which successive Thatcher governments had indulged the defence budget had already been transformed into a more slender diet, and the economic forecasts for the remainder of the decade, whilst moderately encouraging in the short term, are hedged with reservations on a longer perspective, due to fears of rising inflation and a current account deficit on the balance of payments.

Planned British government expenditure 1986-87

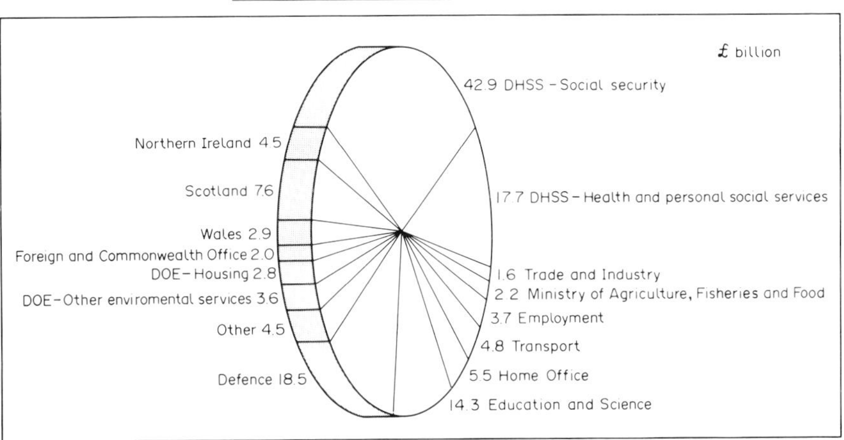

As the pattern of government expenditure for 1986–87 shows, Britain's social security and health budgets will have to be brought under tighter control if Welfare is not to trample triumphantly over Weapons in the struggle for resource allocation. If real increases in British defence spending are ever to be achieved then the "universality" in social policy by which rich and poor alike are entitled to so many of the benefits disbursed by an indulgent state irrespective of the income of the recipient should be modified fundamentally.

Finally, the election of a Labour government could only result in a return to a more severe cycle of defence deprivation for the United Kingdom than even that of 1974–79. Labour's exculpatory claims that the savings which would arise from the decommissioning of the strategic nuclear deterrent force would be switched to increased spending on conventional arms should be discounted. The huge increases in social spending which the Party promises would soon invalidate them. In any case offstage there can again be heard those familiar demands that the level of British defence spending should be no higher than the average of such spending by her main European allies. By whatever yardstick is used, this would produce a defence budget only slightly larger in monetary terms than that of Italy and substantially less than those of France and West Germany. Britain would cease to be in the first division of the European Allies, and her power and influence would decline accordingly.

CHAPTER II

The Politics and Psychology of Defence

A SOUND security policy requires careful co-ordination of defence planning and foreign policy in the enactment of a national strategy in which military, economic, financial and industrial factors are reconciled in the pursuit of long term objectives which are politically attainable. Such a process demands a high degree of national consensus as well as of foresight and interdepartmental co-operation. All are in short supply.

The End of Bipartisanship in Defence

The most profound problem today lies in the breakdown of the unwritten understanding between the principal parties over foreign affairs and defence matters which had characterised politics in Britain since the Second World War. Hitherto the main political differences between the Conservative and Labour Parties have lain over the management of the economy and over the ownership of the means of production, distribution and exchange.

Today British Tories and Socialists have very different views of the world and of Britain's place and role in the international order. There is no precise date from which this divergence occurred, but the change can be clearly traced to the years when Harold Wilson, now Lord Wilson of Rievaulx, was Leader of the Labour Party. The breakdown of bipartisanship on defence particularly gathered momentum during the years when the Labour Party was in Opposition, first under the leadership of Michael Foot and then latterly of Neil Kinnock.

For the first twenty years or so after the end of the World War II, the bipartisanship of wartime and of the Coalition Government of those years was very largely maintained. It was under Clement Attlee's stewardship as the immediate postwar Labour Prime Minister that the United Kingdom's independent nuclear deterrent was created, and it has been maintained by all subsequent Governments.

Just as significantly, its cardinal importance to the security of the United Kingdom was recognised by successive main Opposition Parties. Under

Michael Foot – a veteran of the Campaign for Nuclear Disarmament's Aldermaston marches – and under Neil Kinnock whose wife actively supports CND causes in Britain, the Labour Party moved from a position in Conference critical of a defence strategy dependent on nuclear weapons to the official espousal of a non-nuclear defence policy involving not only the abandonment of the British independent nuclear deterrent but also the closure of United States nuclear bases in Britain.

The Liberal Party, whose Young Liberals organisation has always been radical, could also be experiencing the first stages of the evolution of a climate of opinion within its ranks hostile to nuclear weapons since the emergence in September 1986 of an anti nuclear majority at its Assembly in defiance of the views of the Party Leader, David Steel.

The Social Democratic Party (SDP), whose leading figures are largely drawn from former Labour Party politicians who defected from the Labour Party, in part at least in protest against its growing unilateralism, upholds strongly traditional British postwar defence policy, namely adherence to NATO strategy, including its nuclear element, and the preservation of an independent British nuclear deterrent. Nevertheless the SDP's orthodoxy in matters of national defence adds an element of uncertainty about British security policy on the Centre Left of British politics. The defence policy of the SDP has to be reconciled by a process of some sophistry with the views of its Alliance partners, the Liberals, a process which has been complicated not merely by inter-Party differences of attitude, but by differences too between the Leaders and the led, especially in the Liberal ranks.

As the division in British politics is now so deep, betwen the Conservatives who remain essentially united and free from heresy on defence issues and the Labour Party, which has truly broken the mould of postwar conformity over nuclear strategy, all other questions of security policy receive scant attention. In Parliament unless there is a procurement controversy like the Westland affair or the Nimrod Airborne Early Warning Aircraft fiasco, defence receives little serious attention except from the Defence Select Committee and a handful of specialists on the North Atlantic Assembly and Assembly of Western European Union. With each General Election the number of Members of Parliament with any military experience at all, even of National Service, steadily diminishes.

Public Disinterest in Defence

Members of Parliament are all too representative of their constituents. At Westminster they reflect well in Parliament the preoccupations and aspirations of a largely demilitarised society. For the majority of the British public, armed conflict is an activity observed from the warmth and security of the fireside at home. It takes place entirely on a television screen which either shows films of British derring-do against German Nazi stereotypes or news coverage of real contemporary war, always in far away places and therefore of limited emotional impact.

Seven years of brutal Soviet occupation of Afghanistan have had next to no serious impact on the British public. This torpid response and traditionally British phlegm are totally shared by the peoples of Western Europe as a whole. The fate of neutral Afghanistan should call in question the validity of the slogans of the unilateral disarmers – "*better red than dead*", or "*better a generation of partisan warfare than to risk nuclear retaliation to aggression*," but for most West European people this is not so.

Three or four million refugees from Afghanistan and scores of thousands of dead, maimed and tortured people within the country offer testimony to the perils of neutral propinquity to Soviet Russia. To the list of Finland, Estonia, Latvia, Lithuania and Poland is added in modern days Afghanistan, countries whose sole and fatal common factor in international relations was to have a border with the Soviet Union and a neutral status. Even so the merits of the North Atlantic collective security pact (NATO) and the perils of vulnerability to the Soviet Union are subjects of wide disinterest among a British public all too many of whom view the United States of America – the actual guarantor of British liberty – as great a threat to peace as the Soviet Union.

The Tragedy of Ulster

If wars in far away places like Afghanistan, the Near and Middle East, Africa and Central America seem light years away to the British people, then surely the seventeen-year-old conflict in Ulster must have impinged dramatically on the public consciousness. Not so; inured to the horrors of Ulster violence by the regular desensitising medium of the principal public purveyor of news and opinion, television, most people in Great Britain have remained acquiescent to the troubles in Northern Ireland. After all, did not a respected Conservative Home Secretary speak openly of "*an acceptable level of violence*" and did not a distinguished Secretary of State for Northern Ireland have tea and cakes with leaders of the Irish Republican Army in London's West End? In a sense, the lack of public over-reaction in Britain to Ulster terrorism has been healthy, but it does also permit Governments of the United Kingdom to under-react to the problem and its real implications.

The objective of the IRA was always to destroy the democratic institutions in Northern Ireland. The Parliament of Northern Ireland at Stormont was abolished by the British Government and full local democracy also. The Northern Ireland Assembly was established and then disbanded. At the time of writing, the Anglo-Irish Agreement, a child of wishful thinking in Whitehall, is a year old. The auguries for the future of the Agreement are not good, but neither the British public nor the politicians care, so long as the level of violence remains "*acceptable*". "*All the Irish are mad*", it is said, and "*they all love fighting each other*". It remains to be seen whether hope triumphs over experience about the depth of the sectarian divide in Ulster and whether the Anglo-Irish Agreement will ever be accepted by the loyalist majority.

None the less the United Kingdom has been divided by violence as never before, between Great Britain where essentially traditional democratic institutions persist and the rule of law remains unaltered, and Northern Ireland where Government is enacted by Direct Rule through Orders in Council and where justice is meted out by Diplock Courts without trial by jury.

Although devolved Government may have been abolished in Northern Ireland, security is metaphorically devolved and responsibility for it rests upon the British indigenous mercenaries of the all-Regular Army whose sacrifices pass usually unnoticed and largely unsung in Great Britain and the Royal Ulster Constabulary and Ulster Defence Regiment whose casualty rate would be hard to sustain were not their homes and way of life at risk from a brutal and barbaric enemy whom they at least know must be defeated.

The relative merits and disadvantages of operating an all-Regular Army in support of the Civil Power receive all too little attention. The British public is largely insulated from events in Northern Ireland and the House of Commons, although it has lost three of its Members – Airey Neave, Robert Bradford and Sir Anthony Berry to IRA action, is largely uninterested in the future of a province whose semi-proconsular government is notorious for being a distant graveyard of British political reputations. Were British National Servicemen on duty in West Belfast, South Armagh and the Bogside area of Londonderry, the story wold be very different, so great would be the public clamour for really tough and effective measures against the IRA or for a British withdrawal from Northern Ireland.

As it is there are no votes in Northern Ireland, either literally or figuratively, for any political party in Great Britain. When Edward Heath abolished the Northern Ireland Parliament at Stormont in 1972 the old Conservative and Unionist Party connection was destroyed with the secession of the Ulster Unionists. Now with the imposition of the Anglo-Irish Agreement regardless of the Province-wide by-election verdict against it, the Democratic Unionists and on most occasions nearly all the Official Unionists, except Enoch Powell, have withdrawn from the Westminster Parliament. The most regular attenders are the moderate democratic Republican representatives of the Social Democratic and Labour Party, John Hume and Seamus Mallon. The paradox is complete. Those MPs from Ulster who disavow British jurisdiction in Northern Ireland are by their presence at Westminster the most loyal upholders of the Imperial Parliament, whereas those most frequently absent from Westminster are the most loyal champions of its responsibility under the Crown for the governance of Northern Ireland.

Such are the perverse effects of political violence and terrorism consistently and relentlessly applied as a form of unconventional undeclared warfare to subvert and transform the democratic and judicial institutions of a Province of the State in a manner and to a fashion undesired by the majority of its citizens. It should be re-emphasised that had conscripts from Great Britain been in the front line against the IRA terror campaign, the impact upon public and political opinion would have been rapid and dramatic in its effect.

It is probable that either an Algerian type of political solution would have been found for Northern Ireland or the clear objective set of victory over the IRA rather than its containment. Once set, it would probably have been secured since guerrilla campaigns thrive on political uncertainty and terrorists are sustained by hope, however irrational. The foreclosure of political change in response to terrorism as an option for government and the unequivocal declaration by the authorities that only a zero level of violence was acceptable might well by now have secured the defeat of the IRA.

In these circumstances of total British involvement in the affairs of Northern Ireland through a large presence of conscripts, to take two other analogies, political pressure for either outright victory by means of the mobilisation of all necessary resources as was achieved over the Communist terrorists in Malaya, or of a diplomatic formula as in Cyprus whereby British political responsibility was relinquished while safeguarding British security interests through the establishment of base areas, could perhaps have been secured.

As it is, the Northern Ireland situation is economically a running sore for Britain, the prognosis of which is not good for the political stability of Ireland as a whole. The fact is that, with the notable exception of the recovery of the Falkland Islands in 1982, the British public usually shows little understanding of the need for swift, firm and decisive action in defence matters. When such action is taken as with the air raids by the United States Air Force and Navy against Libya, or with the invasion by United States forces of Grenada, many British people fail to understand its particular justification in either of these instances, or the general threat to Western interests as a whole had developments in either country been allowed to go unchecked.

Public Perceptions and the Rôle of Television

In the case of the Libya raids more people appeared fearful of possible Libyan retaliation than of Libyan sponsored terrorism. In the psychological and hearts and minds campaign which is the concomitant of such operations, broken and maimed children's bodies – the collateral damage of the pre-emptive air attacks – make more dramatic television viewing than arguments in favour of the punishment and deterrence of state sponsored terrorism.

In the case of the American invasion of the Caribbean island of Grenada, the assault on a small and defenceless Commonwealth member country by forces representing the full might of the United States seemed incomprehensible to majority British opinion nurtured on Commonwealth nostalgia and blind to the perils of the further expansion of Marxist influence in the Caribbean basin. Again, pictures of the United States Marine Corps storming ashore to a critical commentary, sometimes from thousands of miles away in London, make better television than does the subsequent peaceful restoration of democracy in an island community where democratic institutions had been highjacked by unscrupulous individuals whose hunger for personal power and Marxist ideology accorded conveniently with the strategic interest in the region of the Soviet Union and its ally Cuba.

Maintaining majority support in the United Kingdom for strong national defences and for full co-operation with Britain's American allies to ensure Western interests is not easy in the television age. It is rendered more difficult by the present lack of bipartisan consensus in these matters. As Britain's power and prestige have declined, so has the nation's sense of isolation grown. The United Kingdom's membership of the European Community is a fact of national economic and political life, yet knowledge of foreign languages is no greater and easier travel to the Continent seems to have brought a minimal improvement of general understanding of European affairs.

In these circumstances it is hard for the few defence conscious politicians in Britain with any significant influence to stimulate a serious debate about Britain's role in the world and the country's security policy. The Brussels Treaty commitment under the Paris Protocols of 1954 to maintain 55,000 men and a Tactical Air Force on the Continent of Europe (in fact in West Germany) is as much a political fact of life as Britain's membership of the EEC and seemingly just as immutable.

There is here a strange ambivalence. Although the United Kingdom is economically and politically more committed to Continental Europe than ever before, and although a dangerous anti-Americanism is manifest in British public opinion, Britain's special relationship with the United States remains very strong – at least as far as the Conservative Party is concerned.

Labour Party Security Policy and American Attitudes

Anxieties about the Labour Party's non-nuclear defence policy have been voiced by the United States Secretary for Defense, Caspar Weinberger, the Supreme Commander Europe General Rogers and Senior Congressional Leaders of the Republican and Democratic Parties alike. Even so, British Labour Party Leaders hope that the United States would acquiesce in the dismantling of American nuclear bases in Britain were a Labour Government to be elected in Britain and would accept a British status within the Alliance similar to that of Greece. Even if the United Kingdom under a Labour Government were to accept United States nuclear equipped forces within British waters, territory or air space in time of war, if not of peace, like Denmark or Norway, the Atlantic Alliance would come under alarming strain. Whether it would actually unravel is an open question, but its political future as an organisation enshrining shared values would be as much in question as its strategy.

The fact is that the British Labour Party is increasingly aligned ideologically and emotionally with political forces hostile to the United States, and is fundamentally out of sympathy with the orientation of United States foreign and security policy worldwide.

On Central America the Labour Party supports the Sandanistas in Nicaragua and deplores assistance on the part of the United States of America to the Contra forces. On South America, the British Labour Party is implacably opposed to General Pinochet's régime in Chile whilst the present United States Administration grants it grudging acquiescence *faute de mieux*. On Southern Africa, most Labour Party supporters would favour the assumption of power, in an independent Namibia by the South West Africa People's Organisation (SWAPO), and disapprove strongly of the operations within Angola of Jonas Savimbi's UNITA forces. In both instances, the reverse is broadly the case as far as United States policy is concerned.

As for the strategically crucial arc of states from the Caucasus to Kashmir, the Labour Party is vehemently out of sympathy with America's staunch allies Turkey and Pakistan. It favours, however, the aspirations of the Palestinian people along the lines of United Nations Security Council Resolution 242 in which proposals for the cession by Israel of territory in return for internationally recognised borders are always considered by the United States and their Israeli allies to be too far reaching.

Looking to the Indian Ocean area and the Pacific, the Labour Party would regard India with particular favour as Kinnock's visit there demonstrated, whereas for the United States, India's excessively close relationship by treaty of Friendship with the USSR reinforced by supplies of sophisticated Soviet armaments poses extreme political and strategic difficulties. Potential Soviet expansionism towards the warm waters of the Gulf, Arabian Sea and Indian Ocean is to the Americans a threat made more real by the Soviet invasion of Afghanistan and the anti-American attitude of India.

In the Pacific the British Labour Party supports the action of Prime Minister Lange's Labour Government in New Zealand whose refusal to grant harbour facilities to United States warships which might be carrying nuclear weapons or which are nuclear powered, has led to the abrogation by the United States of its defensive commitment to New Zealand under the Anzus pact – a precursor of what could happen to Britain under a Labour Government at the hands of a United States administration which might easily decide to revoke its mutual security commitment to Britain under the North Atlantic Treaty if the United Kingdom implemented a non-nuclear defence policy.

Finally, the British Labour Party is unhappy at the authoritarian nature of the South Korean régime which is on friendly terms with its ally and vital security partner, the United States. In the Philippines, the British Labour Party would wish to see the "progressive forces" achieve substantial political change and a process of reform much faster than would the United States. Last but not least, over Indo-China Labour Party spokesmen still speak critically of American involvement in the Viet Nam war more often than they do of the human rights abuses in Campuchea, Laos and Viet Nam after the Communists took power in Indo-China.

All in all, therefore, it is impossible to believe that a British Labour Government could fail to precipitate a major crisis with the United States if it pursued when in office the Party's current defence policies. Across the whole spectrum of international affairs, in all the continents of the globe, and in many aspects of pure defence policy, especially nuclear strategy, current American attitudes and those of the British Labour Party are fundamentally opposed. It is hard to see how the special relationship between Britain and the United States, sanctified as it has been by almost forty years of NATO partnership, could survive such mutual antagonism.

In these circumstances, British Labour leaders should not delude themselves about their influence with United States policy makers. On strategic defence, nuclear testing, the production of binary chemical weapons and anti-satellite weapon systems, as well as over arms control negotiations with the Soviet Union, the United States Government would go its own way even more than it did at the Reykjavik Summit. It would do so heedless of the inhibitions and special pleading of the British Government which, by abrogating the fundamental principles upon which NATO's defence has long been established, would have foresworn the right to be consulted and to influence American policy. Furthermore, any deterioration in the defence relationship between Britain and the USA could only adversely affect the substantial market for British defence equipment in the USA.

By contrast, it would be wrong to imagine that the close understanding in defence matters between the British Government and that of the United States has been primarily based upon the mutual sympathy and respect of President Reagan and Mrs. Thatcher. The excellent personal relations between the two national leaders have been immensely beneficial to the Alliance, but more important is the fact that British security policy is founded on the primacy of the NATO Alliance in national defence priorities and upon a sound adherence to its strategic doctrine.

Of course there have been strains in the Atlantic relationship. The Americans have long felt that the Europeans have assumed too small a share of the common burden of Alliance defence. A particular problem in this respect has been that the Europeans continue to rely on a substantial commitment of some 300,000 United States troops in Europe, yet expect the United States to protect, if necessary by military means, European security interests outside the NATO area also. Furthermore, there are incessant complaints on the part of the Europeans that the so called "two way street" in trade in defence equipment between the United States and Europe has become a one way highway from the United States in the direction of Europe.

If there have been stresses and strains between the European and American components of the North Atlantic Alliance, it might have been expected that the Europeans would seek to forge between themselves a closer identity of interest in defence matters. However, the desire of most European nations to benefit from the enhanced security and lower costs to their national defence budgets which United States forces in Europe and the United States nuclear guarantee provide, outweigh any nascent desire for self-sufficiency or self-assertiveness in defence matters on the part of the Europeans.

Building a European Pillar in the Western Alliance

To these fundamental impediments must be added institutional and political difficulties which seriously hinder the construction of a more integrated Europe in the defence field. European Governments are still keen for the European Community to assert an authority and influence in world affairs commensurate with its undoubted economic importance. However, under the Treaty of Rome, there is no statutory competence for the European Community to arrogate to itself a security policy role. Its members are disparate, ranging from neutral Ireland and neutralist Greece, through Denmark, which participates in the arcane Scandinavian security policy art of the "Nordic Balance", through France and Spain, which are not members of the military organisation of NATO, to the original six of the Common Market plus Britain, which are all signatories of the Brussels Treaty as amended in Paris in 1954 at the time of the collapse of The European Defence Community, and thereby members of Western European Union.

Western European Union was relaunched on the occasion of its thirtieth anniversary at Rome in October 1984. Although the formal process of European Political Co-operation within an EEC framework failed to achieve fully united action against terrorism, owing to the unwillingness of Greece to co-operate, WEU has not been assigned a co-ordinating role in combating international terrorism. Nevertheless, in helping to improve armaments co-operation in Europe and to formulate a joint European response to the

Strategic Defence Initiative, it has potential, especially now that its expert Agencies are being reformed.

However, Governments underfund the WEU's Parliamentary Assembly in Paris which has difficulties enough in not being co-located with the Ministerial Council in London. The hemicycle of the Old Greater London Council Chamber at County Hall would make an ideal replacement for the *Conseil Économique et Social* building in Paris which is used for the Assembly of WEU's part sessions at present. Council, Assembly Secretariat and the expert agencies could all be easily housed under one roof at County Hall, if the British Government and other member Governments had the imagination and the will to see the idea through to fruition and make a truly effective organisation of Western European Union.

Of course, there are other established fora for arms collaboration, like the Independent European Programme Group (IEPG) and the Conference of Armaments Directors (CNAD) at NATO. It would be most helpful to create a constituency in favour of European arms collaboration if the IEPG could report regularly to WEU. The Eurogroup, of which France is not a member, also seeks to co-ordinate the European position within the NATO Alliance as a whole. This role could at least be mirrored by WEU, especially if Portugal, which has applied to join, is allowed to do so. Then, Turkey, Spain and Norway, which currently all send observers to the Parliamentary Assembly of WEU might all apply to join also.

In all these matters, the Europeans must show more vigour in pressing for intiatives. The Franco-German defence treaty is an important bilateral component to strengthening the European pillar of the Atlantic Alliance, just as WEU is an important multilateral component of it also. The military role of Europe beyond the NATO area remains uncertain and unclear, and needs to be concerted. In this respect too, the WEU could be useful. The accession of the NATO flank nations of Turkey and Norway, as well as of the two Iberian nations would give a heightened perception of the perils facing these countries on the extremities of the Alliance, as well as of the importance of seapower.

In conclusion, as Britain, France, and the United States move towards a period of political uncertainty and electrioneering in the next two years, it is very important that political leaders, not just in Britain but throughout Europe, arouse their publics to the problems and imperatives of their common defence. The physical threat from the Soviet Union continues to grow and the public relations skills of First Secretary Gorbachev render the threat even more dangerous. The peoples of Western Europe who have enjoyed peace for two generations can, all too easily, become complacent that their security, which has been so well assured these past forty years, will continue without much sacrifice on their part. This is a dangerous fallacy of which they need to be disabused. Such action will required political leadership and public information skills of the highest order.

CHAPTER III:

Britain and the Bomb

THE possession by the United Kingdom of nuclear weapons is one of the most politically divisive issues in Britain today. It was not always so. In the 1950s and 1960s the Campaign for Nuclear Disarmament's marches to the Aldermaston atomic research establishment were a minority activity featuring such well known personalities of a leftward persuasion as Canon Collins, Michael Foot and Bertrand Russell. They attracted a regular dedicated clientele who were regarded by most of the British population with detached interest but little sense of personal identification or commitment.

The Role of the Peace Movements

Today the Campaign for Nuclear Disarmament and its associated peace movements in Western Europe, with the notable exception of France, have achieved much more than greatly enhanced numerical support. Their aims and purposes have to a considerable extent been translated into the official policy of such respectable parties as the British Labour Party and the West German SPD.

What is more, there is a generalised body of opinion, in addition to the West European Socialist Parties, sympathetic to the aims of CND and the Peace movements, such as the majority of the Liberal Party Assembly in the United Kingdom, many of the rank and file (especially the Young Liberals), most "Greens" in the Federal Republic of Germany, and many non party-political but well intentioned, predominantly young, people in the United Kingdom. These groups act as unwitting agents of influence for those who would wish to see Britain militarily weakened by calling into question the United Kingdom's strategic nuclear deterrent. Astonishingly, they equate the dangers to peace associated with the policies of the democratically elected United States Government with those of the Central Committee of the Communist Party of the Soviet Union. They assert that the United Kingdom faces a heightened risk of attack from the USSR owing to the stationing of United States nuclear forces on British soil, and claim that the United Kingdom's own nuclear deterrent has no strategic value.

In these circumstances there is a major duty upon those who are responsible for the defence of Britain to explain in readily comprehensible terms exactly why the maintenance of a strategic nuclear deterrent on the part of the United Kingdom remains so crucial for European security. One such opportunity exists in the aftermath of the historic and dramatically concluded Summit Meeting in October 1986 in Reykjavik between President Reagan and First Secretary Gorbachev: another will be the forthcoming General Election Campaign in the United Kingdom.

Such a public information campaign has been conducted previously in Britain, in advance of the first deployment of Ground Launched Cruise Missiles (GLCM) at Greenham Common in 1983. Another should now be initiated in favour of the modernisation of the British strategic nuclear deterrent by the procurement of the Trident D5 Submarine Launched Ballistic System (SLBM) from the United States. At the time of writing, a majority undoubtedly exists in the House of Commons in favour of the acquisition of Trident by the United Kingdom, but it is certainly not clear that the merits of this ultimate strategic nuclear deterrent system are judged by most British people to justify its daunting cost, although the majority of the population in the United Kingdom are definitely not unilateralist.

How Independent is the British Deterrent?

Since the signature of the Nassau Agreement in 1962 between Prime Minister Harold Macmillan of the United Kingdom and President John Kennedy of the United States, whereby the United Kingdom procured the Polaris Submarine Launched Ballistic Missile system (SLBM) to replace the V Bomber force of Royal Air Force Bomber Command in the strategic nuclear deterrent role, it has become harder to convince the British public that the British independent strategic nuclear deterrent is truly independent. The United Kingdom has provided the submarines, nuclear devices and ultimately the Chevaline triple warhead for the Polaris SLBM system. For the Trident D5 the United Kingdom will provide once more the nuclear devices and the nuclear submarines (SSBNS), but the independently targeted re-entry vehicles (MIRVs) will be American.

An impression is given of British dependence upon the United States. Indeed it is undeniably true that the United Kingdom remains a strategic nuclear power by courtesy of its American allies. This is in sharp distinction to the French position which rests upon national autonomy and autarchy in all matters of nuclear strategy and deterrence. All three elements of the French triad of the French nuclear deterrent – air to surface stand off missiles, ground launched ballistic missiles, and submarine launched ballistic missile systems – have been manufactured or modernised by French industry from its own national resources in a manner in which the French people can rightly take pride.

There was a time towards the end of the operational life of the V Bomber force in Britain when a joint Franco-British nuclear deterrent could have been realistically envisaged and developed. The Polaris SLBM could even have been accepted as an interim system by the Royal Navy pending the introduction into service of Franco-British nuclear deterrent systems. The current political vulnerability of the proposed British procurement of Trident D5 from the USA would have been avoided and the European pillar of the Alliance greatly strengthened.

As so often, however, in the evolution of European security policy, a key opportunity was missed which recent European defence policy initiatives on the part of the Alliance between the Liberal and the Social Democratic Parties in Britain seem unlikely to be able to redress since, at this late stage, British participation in the French independent nuclear deterrent is not really technically or politically possible. The vague and ill-defined ideas of a Franco-British nuclear deterrent mooted by Liberal and SDP leaders in Britain are addressed more to reconciling the nuclear strategies of their respective Parties than to offering a practical means of modernising the two European national deterrents.

In short, in few areas of public policy does the special relationship of the United Kingdom with the United States of America manifest itself with greater clarity or consequence than over the maintenance of Britain's strategic nuclear deterrent. It has to be understood how special that Anglo/American relationship is over nuclear strategy since it has major implications for the security of the United States as well as for Britain.

Although the British strategic nuclear deterrent is no longer truly autonomous and although it is normally assigned to the Supreme Allied Commander Europe (SACEUR), the United Kingdom Government reserves to itself the right to independent use of the United Kingdom's strategic nuclear forces if the sovereignty, independence, liberty and national security of the British nation and people are imperilled in a manner which cannot be redressed in the context of the collective security provisions of the North Atlantic Treaty.

The Importance of French and British Nuclear Forces

The maintenance of such a centre of independent nuclear decision in the United Kingdom, as in France, enhances the overall credibility of Western deterrence. An additional element of uncertainty is injected into a potential aggressor's calculation of the response to be expected to its aggression on the part of the Western Alliance and from two key European members of that Alliance in particular and not just from the United States. Furthermore, the United States' nuclear guarantee to Western Europe is enhanced by the maintenance of the French and British national nuclear deterrents, because their independent invocation in retaliation to an act of aggression which did not at the outset provoke an American nuclear response, would almost certainly precipitate an escalating process or trigger effect leading ultimately to United States nuclear retaliation on behalf of its European allies. Once a nuclear exchange was initiated in Europe, it would be hard for the United States to stand aloof.

The French and British nuclear deterrents therefore strengthen the coupling between the European and United States elements of the Alliance, and make a contribution to the security of Britain and France as well as to Western Europe as a whole out of all proportion to their size and cost. Both are however minimum deterrents.

Arms Control and the British Deterrent

Whereas the Soviet General Secretary, Mikhail Gorbachev, agreed specially, for the purpose of the Iceland Summit, to exclude the French and British strategic nuclear deterrent forces from the discussions between the Soviet Union and the United States over strategic nuclear weapons limitation, and since they have not featured in the arms control negotiations at Geneva between the two Superpowers, it is noteworthy that the French and British Governments have adopted similar but by no means identical public positions over the superpower arms control talks and the possible relevance of those negotiations to their respective national nuclear deterrents.

For the French Government, France's nuclear forces represent a totally non-negotiable symbol of the French nation's sovereignty and independence. It is a clear and unexceptionable position from the strategic point of view. For the United Kingdom Government, the British strategic deterrent is more of a minimum deterrent than that of France, since it relies on a single submarine based delivery system and not a triad of different systems. Nevertheless, the British Government has stated that if there is spectacular progress in the field of arms control leading to substantial mutual reductions in strategic offensive nuclear systems and a more stable, balanced deterrent regime marked by a sense of enhanced security and international confidence on both sides, then the British nuclear deterrent force could be included in the East–West arms control process.

This was made clear by the British Secretary of State for Foreign Affairs, Sir Geoffrey Howe, in his statement of 5 November 1986 at the Conference on Security and Co-operation in Europe Review Meeting in Vienna:

> *"I have clearly set out many times the position of the British nuclear deterrent including to Mr. Shevardnadze himself. If Soviet and United States strategic arsenals were to be very substantially reduced and no significant changes had occurred in Soviet defensive capabilities, Britain would want to review her position and to consider how best she could contribute to arms control in the light of the reduced threat. In short we have never said never."*

However, the British inventory of four Polaris nuclear submarines and of ultimately four Trident submarines is so minimal that it is hard to see how it could ever safely be included in any superpower arms control negotiation. Even if Soviet intermediate range nuclear forces (SS20s) were totally eliminated from Europe, the threat from such short range systems as the SS21, SS22 and SS23 would remain.

With four submarines in service it is always possible for the Royal Navy to keep at least one nuclear ballistic missile submarine (SSBN) on station. Any reduction in the overall number of SSBNs in the Royal Navy's inventory would eliminate the United Kingdom as a totally credible nuclear power in the strategic deterrent field. The potential threat to the United Kingdom does not derive solely from the USSR's nuclear forces, grave as this is. The formidable Warsaw Pact capability for chemical and biological warfare needs also to be considered. Furthermore a number of countries other than the USSR could eventually also threaten the United Kingdom with nuclear weapons. Keeping a deterrent to such an eventuality is an essential British interest.

In case such nuclear proliferation were to occur, it would be foolish for the Government of the United Kingdom to relinquish a British capacity to exercise strategic nuclear deterrence or response on its own behalf to any nuclear threat, intimidation or blackmail from whatsoever quarter. Whereas the Soviet nuclear threat to Britain may be by far the largest, it is by no means the only one.

Naturally the Soviet Union has an interest in encouraging unilateralist tendencies within British political and public opinion. The closure of United States nuclear bases in Britain would undoubtedly cause a crisis of confidence within the Western Alliance as it would be an action on the part of the United Kingdom tantamount to a unilateral renunciation of British participation in the nuclear element of NATO's strategy of flexible response.

The American nuclear guarantee has offset the unwillingness of the European members of NATO to spend enough to provide fully effective conventional defences against the massed, in place formations of the Warsaw Pact which could operationally be expected to have the formidable advantage of surprise. It is impossible to exaggerate the importance to Western Europe's security of maintaining the US nuclear guarantee. The more divided the Western Alliance, the higher the probability that the Soviet Union might be tempted to initiate military adventures in Western Europe.

The Dangers of British Unilateral Disarmament

There have been suggestions on the part of Moscow that if a future British Government eliminated the sixty four Polaris missiles from the United Kingdom's inventory, then the Soviets would be prepared to reduce comparably their own offensive nuclear missiles on a direct one for one basis. This would mean that when the United Kingdom had exercised a unilateral zero option of its own, the Soviet offensive missile arsenal would have been cut from about 10,000 to 9,936. This would be a negligible contribution to make towards arms control worldwide. In return the vulnerability of the United Kingdom would be dramatically enhanced.

In these circumstances the British Labour Party's spokesmen have insisted that they would not wish the United Kingdom, once it had unilaterally renounced its own strategic nuclear deterrent, to shelter under the United States nuclear umbrella. US nuclear bases in Britain would be closed and United States and NATO nuclear forces forced to withdraw from the United Kingdom. "If we're not prepared to use the nuclear weapon ourselves," the Labour Party Leader, Neil Kinnock, declared on 28 September 1986, "*We certainly would not be asking anyone else to jeopardise themselves by the use of that nuclear weapon. I think it would be immoral to do so.*"[1] Since then there have been some murmurings of qualification to this posture of high-minded defencelessness from Labour spokesmen, indicating that if returned to office, a Labour Government might prove less than anxious to throw away the American shield.

It must be said that such a policy of total vulnerability is naïve in the extreme and ignores the principal fact that, in safeguarding its own strategic interests, the United States would use all appropriate means to do so, including the nuclear option, regardless of the attitudes struck by the British Labour Party, moral or otherwise. The United States could still invoke nuclear retaliation to prevent Warsaw Pact forces invading Britain in the event of war. The United States Government might judge that if the British Isles were to fall to the Warsaw Pact, the balance of power in the North Atlantic Basin would be dramatically shifted in favour of the Soviet Union and the security of vital American interests, as well as of the United States themselves, jeopardised. Whether any United States Administration could permit such an eventuality is extremely doubtful. It seems certain that all appropriate responses by the United States would be bound to be considered, including a nuclear one, if necessary over the head of a nuclear-free and influence-free British Government.

Likewise, making the United Kingdom a nuclear-free zone would not guarantee immunity from Warsaw Pact attack any more than the neutrality of the Soviet Union's immediate neighbours, Afghanistan, Finland, Estonia, Latvia, Lithuania and Poland, prevented acts of Soviet aggression against them. Indeed, if history has a lesson, it is that geographical propinquity and military vulnerability have proved a stimulus to Soviet aggressive tendencies rather than the contrary. That is why senior United States spokesmen from the Secretary for Defence downwards have outspokenly criticised the irresponsibility of the Labour Party's policy on nuclear weapons and argued that its implementation would have a deeply damaging effect on the NATO Alliance.

It has been the unity of all members of the Atlantic Alliance behind a common strategy of flexible response and above all the ultimate United States nuclear guarantee which have kept the peace in Western Europe.

Since the signature of the North Atlantic Treaty in 1949, the Soviet Union has invaded its Warsaw Pact Allies Hungary and Czechoslovakia in 1956 and 1968 respectively and its neutral neighbour Afghanistan in 1979 but, significantly, no NATO country to date.

The Soviet Union has encouraged a radical Marxist orientation to revolutions in non-aligned countries like Angola, Ethiopia and Nicaragua by the provision of material assistance but NATO countries have not been subjected to such outright Soviet subversion. To call in question a highly successful strategy on the part of the North Atlantic Alliance by means of a unilateral British renunciation of nuclear weapons is not merely irresponsible, but so dangerous as to be malign.

Arms Control After the Reykjavik Summit

Of course Britain's nuclear deterrent cannot be regarded as a totally fixed, immutable constant regardless of the global strategic situation, major changes in the international order or balance of power, and developments in arms control and disarmament negotiations between the superpowers. As the Prime Minister said when opening the debate on the Queen's Speech on 12 November 1986:

> *"The significance of Reykjavik is that after many years of talking about arms control, there is now a prospect of major arms reductions – provided that the Soviet Union does not make agreement on all arms control measures dependent on others accepting the constraints it wants to put on the Strategic Defence Initiative."*[2]

The President of the United States' vision on arms control matters has always been more futuristic than that of the British Government, ever since his speech to the American people of 23 March, 1983 announcing the Strategic Defence Initiative when he asked "*Would it not be better to save lives than to avenge them and set through strategic defensive systems the goal of 'lasting stability'?*". In his television address of 13 October 1986 after the Reykjavik Summit, President Reagan referred to the request of the Soviets for a ten-year delay in the deployment of SDI programmes and continued:

> *"In an effort to see how we could satisfy their concerns while protecting our principles and security, we proposed a 10-year period in which we began with the reduction of all strategic nuclear arms, bombers, air-launched cruise missiles, intercontinental ballistic missiles, submarine launched ballistic missiles and the weapons they carry. They would be reduced 50 per cent in the first 5 years. During the next 5 years, we would continue by eliminating all remaining offensive ballistic missiles, of all ranges. During that time we would proceed with research, development and testing of SDI. All done in conformity with ABM provisions. At the 10-year point, with all ballistic missiles eliminated, we could proceed to deploy advanced defenses, at the same time permitting the Soviets to do likewise.*
>
> *"Here the debate began. The General Secretary wanted wording that in effect would have kept us from developing the SDI and unless I agreed, all that work toward eliminating nuclear weapons would go down the drain – cancelled.*
>
> *"I told him I had pledged to the American people that I would not trade away SDI – there was no way I could tell our people their government would not protect them against nuclear*

destruction. I went to Reykjavik determined that everything was negotiable except two things, our freedom and our future."

Arms Control and Strategic Defence

The phrase "*everything was negotiable*" must have caused consternation in Whitehall. The British Foreign Office has always been sceptical about the Strategic Defence Initiative. The first public reaction in a speech by the Foreign Secretary, Sir Geoffrey Howe, to the Royal United Services Institute for Defence Studies on 15 March 1985 begged more questions than it answered.[3] Since then the United Kingdom Ministry of Defence has signed a Memorandum of Understanding with the United States Department of Defence for the participation by British industrial companies and Government Research Establishments in research programmes related to the Strategic Defence Initiative. Nevertheless, the industrial and technical benefits of British participation in SDI are one thing: the strategy another. The idea voiced by President Reagan in his same television address of 13 October 1986 that "*if the program (SDI) was practical we would both eliminate our offensive missiles and then we would share the benefits of advanced defences*" must have heightened British anxieties. It can, of course, be argued that the elimination of the strategic nuclear threat would increase the danger of some form of conventional adventurism on the part of the Warsaw Pact.

First, a minimum nuclear deterrent like the British one depends for its effectiveness on a total vulnerability to ballistic missile attack on the part of the Soviets inherent in their maintenance of a nuclear deterrent doctrine of mutual assured destruction – in other words, the existing balance of terror between the Superpowers.

For the United States Administration strategic defences hold the promise, as described in Assistant Secretary for Defense Richard Perle's interview of 14 October 1986 after the Reykjavik Summit, "*of a far safer and more stable world, a world unburdened by offensive ballistic missiles in which defenses could serve to ensure us both against third world countries that might acquire these missiles and would ensure the free world against Soviet cheating*". For the British Government wholly reliant on the procurement of Trident D5 from the United States of America to remain a strategic nuclear power, such an international order could mark the end of an era when Britain's small but significant offensive nuclear capability could be judged capable of penetrating the heartland of the Soviet Union and wreaking a level of damage on specific targets out of all proportion to the potential benefits to the Soviets of aggression.

Secondly, if in President Reagan's words on television on 13 October 1986 "*both sides seemed willing to find a way to reduce even to zero the strategic ballistic missiles we have aimed at each other*", serious consequences would ensue for the British independent nuclear deterrent. If General Secretary Gorbachev's Press Conference statement of the day before can be taken at face value that his Government's proposals on strategic weapons limitation were tabled at Reykjavik "*with the intention that by the end of this century this most lethal form of weapon (the ballistic missile) would be completely eliminated*", then indeed the Soviets were proposing "*really major steps, deep reductions and not cosmetic steps appropriate to a time when bold, responsible actions in the interests of the whole world, including the peoples of the Soviet Union and the USA, are needed.*"

The Future of the British Trident System

Although such purple prose was probably uttered by Gorbachev with its propaganda effect on an over-optimistic public opinion particularly in Western Europe very much in mind, the assonance of the respective statements on the broad themes of arms control and disarmament by the two Superpower leaders at Reykjavik must put in doubt the determination of the United States Government, particularly of a successor Administration to that of Ronald Reagan, perhaps of the Democratic rather than Republican Party, to implement the agreement with the United Kingdom to sell to Britain the Trident D5 SLBM. This would be notwithstanding Gorbachev's further Press Conference statement on the question of French and British missiles in general "*to leave it to one side . . . and let them remain as an independent force, let them increase and be further improved*".

The fact is that in Milkhail Gorbachev's words of 12 October again "there is already an agreed concept, idea on this subject" of what the General Secretary called "well and honestly balanced reductions in the structure of strategic armed forces that have come about historically". The trouble is that the future of the British strategic nuclear deterrent is not particularly relevant to these agreed concepts and understandably the British Prime Minister sought clarification on the attitude of the United States Government in a meeting with President Reagan at Camp David in mid November 1986. Essentially, Prime Minister Thatcher obtained all she wanted, and in particular an agreement with President Reagan that priority must be given to an INF agreement with restraints on shorter range systems; a 50 per cent cut over five years in US and Soviet strategic offensive weapons and a ban on chemical weapons.

For the British Prime Minister facing a General Election before July 1988 at the latest, the key paragraph was the last one:-

> *"The President reaffirmed the United States' intention to proceed with its strategic modernisation programme, including Trident. He also confirmed his full support for the arrangements made to modernise Britain's independent nuclear deterrent with Trident."*[4]

Alternatives to Trident

Arguments still persist as to whether the Trident D5 is the optimum strategic nuclear deterrent system for the United Kingdom. Even as recently as 13 November 1986 in the debate on the Address in the House of Lords, Admiral of the Fleet Lord Lewin had to explain that to run on the Royal Navy's Polaris force beyond its planned replacement date is not feasible, both for hull life considerations of the submarines and from the point of view of the reliability of the Polaris A3 missiles themselves, which have long since been out of service and out of production in the United States. In short Lord Lewin stated that "*it would be culpably irresponsible from a professional viewpoint to plan on running the Polaris force beyond 1995*".[5]

Likewise cruise missiles would not be an effective substitute whether sea launched, ground or even air launched. Modern air defences, including Airborne Early Warning and fighter forces with look down/shoot down capabilities, make such systems increasingly vulnerable. Their relatively short range is a further disadvantage compared with Trident, which has fifteen times more sea room in the vastness of the oceans in which to hide compared with Polaris, itself a much longer range offensive system than any cruise missile.

Admiral of the Fleet Lord Lewin concluded his authoritative speech by declaring:

> *"The Alliance policy to cancel Trident but to maintain the deterrent may have electoral attraction. However, I believe that it would be more honest and more realistic to accept that if Polaris is to be replaced then Trident is the only replacement."*[6]

Finally, each Trident missile can take between one and fourteen warheads and there are sixteen missile tubes per submarine. The British Government has not yet made public any decision on how many warheads each Trident SSBN would carry, so there is no question of its procurement being an irresponsible proliferation of offensive nuclear delivery systems by the British Government. As Lord Lewin so convincingly summarised the position,

> *"The maximum potential of the one submarine which can be kept on station from a four-submarine force, is 224 missiles – not the 500-plus which are so often quoted. However, the number of missiles that are bought; the number of missiles that are put into tubes; the number of tubes that are left empty; and the number of warheads that are put on each missile is a ministerial option and a decision that does not have to be taken yet. The Alliance say that they will maintain a minimum deterrent. Trident is as minimum as Ministers may care to make it."*[7]

The Intermediate and Short Range Missile Equations

No commentary on the British independent nuclear deterrent would be complete without a mention of theatre nuclear weapons, offensive systems of intermediate range which can strike targets throughout Europe and not beyond. Now that the United Kingdom, unlike France, no longer has an independent national theatre nuclear capability following the disbandment of the Royal Air Force's force of Vulcan bombers, NATO's own intermediate range nuclear forces of Ground Launched Cruise Missiles and Pershing II rockets assume an even greater importance in securing the essential coupling on the ladder of nuclear escalation between NATO's tactical nuclear weapons in Europe and the United States' strategic nuclear deterrent.

The idea mooted at Reyjkavik of an elimination (zero/zero reduction) of intermediate range nuclear forces both by NATO and the Warsaw Pact has grave dangers for NATO in view of the nine to one superiority in short range systems (SS21, SS22 and SS23 missiles) on the part of the Warsaw Pact, in addition to its preponderance in conventional forces and chemical warfare capability. The Supreme Commander Europe, General Bernard Rogers, expressed his anxieties to the North Atlantic Assembly meeting in Istanbul in November 1986 when he said that an agreement to eliminate medium range missiles from Europe "*would leave NATO in a worse position than it was in seven years ago*", that is before the two-track NATO decision of 1979.

A zero-zero option was less risky for NATO before its own modernisation of its INF began in December 1983, that is before the build up of SS21s, SS22s and SS23s in East Germany and Czechoslovakia began. This build up should be an impetus towards the establishment in Western Europe of Anti Tactical Ballistic Missile systems (ATBMs), perhaps technically the most immediately practicable part of an overall strategic defence system. From the arms control point of view, a most prudent policy on INF was enunciated by the Prime Minister of the United Kingdom in the debate on the Address on 12 November, 1986:-

> *"The Government would support the conclusion of an intermediate nuclear forces agreement, which would set limits on medium-range nuclear missiles or even eliminate all such weapons in Europe and the western Soviet Union. But such an agreement must be accompanied by credible and effective verification; strict limits on Soviet SS20s in the Far East; and by agreement on how to deal with shorter-range nuclear missiles, of which the Soviet Union has many more than NATO – and it is worth remembering that large areas of Britain are within range of those weapons."*[8]

CHAPTER IV

Defence and Democracy

ONE of the most challenging problems facing democracies is how to preserve popular support for national defence. Autocracies and dictatorships have an advantage over democratically elected governments in that they can harness more readily the resources of the state to military purposes. Democracies are typefied by recognised political oppositions, constitutional checks and balances and the regular alternation of power. These characteristics, while efficient in preserving individual liberties within the state, are not so efficient in time of peace in mobilising for military objectives the essential ingredients of national defence, namely adequate manpower, industrial potential and finance as well as most importantly of all, favourable public opinion.

The Spectrum of Threats to Freedom

Today the threats to the preservation of Britain's democratic liberties and the rule of law are more wide ranging yet more intense than for many years. At one end of the spectrum, that of violent alienation from society and political subversion, the incidence of politically motivated violent crime and terrorist outrages is infinitely higher than a generation ago. Mass picketing has been used to transform the traditional process of peaceful assembly and trade union bargaining into an exercise in violent cajolery and often brutal intimidation. Terrorism is an international scourge throughout many countries in Western Europe which has cost France, West Germany, Italy, Spain and the United Kingdom alone hundreds of millions of pounds in physical damage and expenditure on security measures.

Conventional warfare remains a potentially credible option for the Soviet Union, primarily outside the geographical limits of the North Atlantic Treaty area, but also conceivably within the NATO area probably for very limited objectives which could be gained by surprise attack or coup de main tactics. The need for effective conventional defence in the nuclear age is too little understood in the United Kingdom which, owing to the cost effectiveness of its nuclear deterrent, has been able to secure its national defence for the last generation without the social cost of conscription. The percentage of men of military age in the armed forces in Britain is lower than that of most comparable countries.

Finally, the arms control process, whose purpose is continued deterrence at a lower level of nuclear armaments on either side, gives the public the impression that the Western priority is the reduction of nuclear stockpiles for its own sake rather than as an enhancement of national security. Too many politicians and commentators so overstress the importance of nuclear disarmament that they underemphasise or ignore the Soviet nuclear build up.

At the Reykjavik Summit meeting in October 1986 even the President of the United States was inadvertantly guilty of sustaining the wildly over optimistic hopes of the protagonists of nuclear disarmament by opening up the prospect of massive cuts in intermediate range and strategic nuclear missiles between the Superpowers. General Secretary Gorbachev did everything possible to sustain this optimism by citing the continuation of the United States Stragegic Defence Initiative as the sole impediment to such dramatic arms reductions. Furthermore, the general public remains largely ignorant of the daunting preponderance in chemical weapons on the part of the Soviets, and neither the politicians nor the media in the West do much to disabuse them of their ignorance.

The Role of Parliament and Public Opinion

In Britain, those politicians who care for national defence have a difficult task in winning the struggle for the hearts and minds of the electorate against the protagonists of unilateral disarmament and the peace movements. Public opinion is swayed largely by television. Parliamentary debates receive little attention from the mass of the population except on the really big historic occasions, but the visual images of television, especially if maintained on a particular theme over a long period of time, have a powerful opinion forming effect. When viewed on television, demonstrations, peaceful protests, candlelight vigils and human chains around nuclear bases all conjure up strong mental images, as advocates of one-sided disarmament by the United Kingdom comprehend and utilise to the full. Most House of Commons speeches by contrast pass almost unnoticed in the House of Commons itself, let alone outside it. The cut and thrust of Prime Minister's Question Time, an event of political theatre, is reported extensively, serious speeches much less.

If Parliament, therefore, is to exert any significant influence in these crucial matters of defence and security policy, it must adapt itself and its role so that people's elected representatives can be seen to shape strategic policy more effectively. At present there are relatively few big set piece defence debates during the parliamentary year. There is one two-day debate on the Defence Estimates which allows members of Parliament to discuss the overall strategy set out in the Annual Defence White Paper. Even this is much taken up with local issues – constituency speeches, not strategy.

There are three individual single Service days, one for the Royal Navy, one for the Army and one for the Royal Air Force. Finally there is a short debate on the Navy, Army and Air Force Discipline Acts continuation orders which comes on late at night. In addition there are short debates on Private Members' motions, the Consolidated Fund or the Adjournment introduced by individual backbenchers but they carry little weight.

In the House of Lords the defence debates are better informed and generally more authoritative owing to the participation of former Chiefs of Staff, retired senior Service officers, ex-Ambassadors, top civil servants and Chairmen of major industrial companies. Even so the authority of past offices held and the wisdom of accumulated years cannot compensate for the fact that the Upper House remains essentially a chamber for reconsideration and amendment with little influence upon public opinion. Lacking the crucial power to vote funds, its effect upon military strategy is small, although the speeches of some peers on defence matters, such as Field Marshal Lord Carver on nuclear strategy or of Lord Chalfont on strategic defence, merit very careful study by policy makers and academic experts alike. The quality of defence debates in the House of Lords is much higher than of those in the House of Commons, but their impact is probably less.

The Role of the Defence Select Committee

The Select Committee on Defence has enhanced the standing of Parliament as the ultimate arbiter of the expenditure of public finance. Its reports are comprehensive, well researched and often indispensable, unclassified reading on major defence issues. The reports which it submitted to the House on the Westland Affair exposed frankly and objectively the errors and failures of policy which culminated in the political crisis over the Christmas/New Year period of 1985-86. At the end of 1986, it seemed likely that another such post-mortem would be initiated by the House of Commons Select Committee on Defence on the cancellation of the Nimrod Mk3 Airborne Early Warning aircraft and the procurement for the Royal Air Force of the Boeing E3A Sentry Airborne Early Warning and Control System (AWACS).

However, a much more fruitful role for the Defence Select Committee would lie in the stimulation of potentially fruitful policy initiatives for the future rather than in inquests into past failures. The Select Committee should be sensitive to the public mood and by the early identification of problems and opportunities to be tackled by the Ministry of Defence, offer periodically to Government an institutional mechanism more responsive to the defence needs of the country than the bureaucracy of the Ministry of Defence with its overriding responsbility as the executor of policy.

The Need for a Defence Equipment Appropriations Sub-Committee

In Britain the most dramatic political controversies in the field of defence occur over procurement issues – the cancellation of TSR2 and Nimrod AEW Mark 3, the future of the Westland company and associated policy for the purchase of helicopters for the Armed Forces, the decision to buy Trident D5 today or in the 1960s to phase out Britain's conventional strike aircraft carriers. Yet understanding of such technical questions among the electorate's democratically elected representatives is even less than it is over general defence matters. This is partly because few MPs have a technical background, or even industrial, let alone military, experience. Ideally all three are required for a fully informed comprehension of the problems of identifying and fulfilling military requirements efficiently, economically and profitably and in a manner which brings the community the industrial benefits of assured and rewarding employment, and to the Armed Forces the weapons they need at a cost the country can afford.

A corpus of parliamentary specialists in this key field would greatly improve the quality of debate and the questioning of Defence Ministers in the House of Commons. The best way to achieve it would be by establishing a Defence Equipment Appropriations Sub-Committee of the House of Commons Select Committee on Defence. Its members would be required to obtain appropriate official security clearance. The Sub-Committee would possess the traditional Select Committee power to call for persons and papers, but significantly the Ministry of Defence would be required to be far more open over its currently ultra secretive process of procuring defence equipment, at the very least when under examination by the Equipment Appropriations Sub-Committee.

The Excessive Secrecy of the Ministry of Defence

At present the Ministry of Defence refuses to publish the rival bids when tenders are issued for proposals from industry to meet a particular military requirement. This is in evident contradiction to the Ministry of Defence's much publicised official policy of obtaining better value for money in the procurement of defence equipment by maximising competition for contracts. It is very different from the procedure in the United States which is far more open. Such excessive British Government secrecy cannot be justified realistically on security grounds and can undermine public confidence in decision making over armament purchases on the part of the Ministry of Defence.

For example the Shorts Tucano was selected as the new basic trainer for the Royal Air Force to succeed the Jet Provost in preference to the Pilatus PC9 aircraft. Parliament and public were informed that the savings to the Ministry of Defence were considerable. However, how could this be proved without the figures and how could an informed judgment be made of the relative merits of the two aircraft by those who have to approve the cost, namely MPs, without the appropriate information?

The need, therefore, for a Defence Equipment Appropriations Sub-Committee is clear. Such information as the capital and life cycle costs of contending weapon systems, relative performance (in broad terms), and related questions such as the type of contract, performance incentives and penalty clauses would all be considered, if necessary in closed session. A report could be prepared for the Select Committee as a whole and for the whole House, declassified as necessary, so that the House of Commons would have the relevant facts before Parliament was called upon to endorse the selection of an equipment item of major importance for the Armed Forces. Much of the current high political drama would rightly be removed from what should be, and should be seen to be, the wholly rational process of equipment selection.

There is at present no parliamentary mechanism in Britain, unlike in the USA, for writing in or deleting particular items from the Defence Budget. Nor should it be advocated now for the United Kingdom. Insufficient consensus across Party lines exists to make such a system operable. The pacifist-neutralist wing of the Parliamentary Labour Party is so doctrinally and emotionally removed from other Members of Parliament on the Centre and Right of the political spectrum that the whole process would probably become a hopeless political dogfight. Undoubtedly, the ordering of defence equipment is too sensitive and important a business to be totally vulnerable to the emotions and vagaries of parliamentary politics, but it does merit careful scrutiny on a routine basis by a select group of parliamentary specialists.

As so often in such potentially controversial questions of public policy, there is a balance of political, military, industrial and commercial interests to be struck which Parliament itself in consultation with the Ministry of Defence should be able to resolve. Above all, the British Parliament and people could benefit from far earlier detailed appreciations and open analyses on the defence equipment needs of the British Armed Forces.

To take some recent examples, the House of Commons, and through it the British public, could have been made aware of the weakness in the United Kingdom's air defences from a lack of Early Warning Aircraft and from the failure of the Nimrod AEW Mark 3 to meet the Royal Air Force specification. So, too, could a Defence Equipment Appropriations Sub-Committee have identified well in advance the failure of the Ministry of Defence to order more helicopters in time to avert the Westland crisis. Finally, the need for the Royal Navy to operate V/STOL Harrier aircraft for the Invincible class of through deck cruisers could have been foreseen much earlier.

Intelligent anticipation, political early warning and analysis of problems to come or issues to be addressed in the future should be the task of the Defence Select Committee as a whole and not just of the Appropriations Sub-Committee. At the present time it could usefully study the merits or otherwise of conscription, the need for a Defence Review to match Defence commitments to projected budgetary resources, the implications for deterrence of strategic defence, the possible effects on European security of INF reductions and the related issue of the build up of Soviet short range nuclear systems in Eastern Europe.

These are some of the initiatives taken in a national context by the House of Commons Defence Select Committee which could restore to the parliamentary processes of the House as a whole the primacy of responsibility for the nation's strategic interests as well as for the careful scrutiny and monitoring of expenditure for the country's defence. However, defence is a supremely international business. Britain's national integrity, sovereignty and independence are assured by the collective security of the NATO Alliance, yet international parliamentary collaboration to secure an international constituency of well informed legislators to support the common security of the Alliance which transcends national interests and local considerations, is insufficiently effective.

International Assemblies

There are essentially two needs at a parliamentary level, both of which are to some extent met by existing international Assemblies. First the need to ensure that senior parliamentarians within the NATO Alliance comprehend NATO strategy, support its objectives and lend their political backing to the Alliance's collective security provisions. The North Atlantic Assembly fulfils this requirement admirably. It has no executive powers but it plays an important advisory and deliberative political role on behalf of the Alliance as a whole and its importance should not be underestimated.

Recently the stresses and strains within the Alliance have been more political than military, for example, over the twin track decision in 1979 for INF modernisation through the deployment of Ground Launched Cruise Missiles (GLCM) and Pershing II ballistic missiles; over the potential impact of the Strategic Defence Initiative on the arms control process; over burden sharing – whether the European members of NATO contribute enough to the common defence of the Alliance. For all these reasons, a genuinely Atlantic-wide forum, such as The North Atlantic Assembly, is invaluable to secure better understanding by parliamentarians of their colleagues' respective national and political views.

The other requirement is to ensure that the European dimension of the defence of the Western Alliance is better concerted and agreed. The "European pillar" of NATO evidently needs to be strengthened. First if the United States is to comprehend European attitudes to security policy questions, those attitudes must be harmonised and agreed. Otherwise a plethora of disparate opinions and unco-ordinated viewpoints on the part of the European members of the Alliance will diminish further United States confidence in the resolve and unity of NATO. The Eurogroup within NATO is a necessary and well proven body which owes its existence to the evident need of the European countries of NATO to achieve an improved degree of concertation of policy in the defence field. However, without France's participation, the Eurogroup is effectively weakened, although the French do take part in the work both of the Conference of National Armaments Directors (CNAD) and of the Independent European Programme Group to co-ordinate action with its allies over weapons procurement.

All these bodies are worthwhile and fulfil essential functions, but all lack the key ingredient which is a political dimension so as to involve people's elected representatives and thereby influence public opinion. It is the growing apathy towards defence matters within Western Europe which is so disquieting. With its unique combination of a Ministerial Council in London that involves Foreign and Defence Ministers as well as permanent representatives of the member countries, together with specialist agencies of experts in the fields of arms collaboration and arms control in Paris with a Parliamentary Assembly in the same building, Western European Union (WEU) has real potential if it is imaginatively exploited.

Western European Union – The Need for Revitalisation

The revivification in 1984 of the Western European Union announced by the Ministerial Council in Rome on the occasion of the 30th Anniversary of the signature of the Paris protocols could have a dramatic effect on the long moribund organisation, but the high hopes for its future will wither into disappointment and frustration unless further action is taken soon.

The historic speech of the French Prime Minister, Jacques Chirac to the Assembly of the WEU in December, 1986, momentarily put WEU at the centre of the European stage for the discussion of security policy. The speech to the same part session by the Secretary General of NATO, Lord Carrington, demonstrated that an active WEU is beneficial to NATO rather than the contrary. Both the Secretary General of NATO and the French Prime Minister identified valuable roles for this body in promoting enhanced armaments collaboration within Europe and a concertation of policy on strategic defence.

These two roles, whilst entirely laudable, are not exactly innovative. The Assembly of WEU has been preaching the merits of such collaboration almost since its foundation over thirty years ago. The paramount necessity of achieving more progress in this field has been well exemplified during the Westland and Nimrod affairs in the United Kingdom. There is much loose talk in WEU about associating the Assembly more closely with the work of the Independent European Programme Group (IEPG). At present the officials of the IEPG report entirely to the national Ministries of Defence from which they originate. There is regrettably as yet no mechanism for subjecting the Chairman in office of the IEPG to questioning from the Assembly of WEU or for him to give a progress report to the Assembly.

On the question of the Strategic Defence Initiative the Assembly of WEU pressed long and hard for its Council to examine what the effect of the successful development of effective strategic defence systems by the United States of American could be on Europe's security, on the maintenance of deterrence within the continent of Europe, on arms control and on the relationship between the superpowers. At long last some study work into these issues is being pursued within the ambit of WEU but key members of the organisation, like the United Kingdom, Italy and Germany, have concluded their own individual agreements with the USA and gone their own national ways on industrial participation.

Concentration of all the organs of Western European Union, Council, Parliamentary Assembly and Specialist Agencies in one presitigious location, preferably the old County Hall in London, would help focus public attention on the problems and imperatives of European defence. However it is not so much rational organisation or administrative convenience which will make Western European Union into an effective body, important as they are, but the quality of the personnel.

The Ministerial Council of Defence and Foreign Ministers, should seek to meet at full Ministerial level as much as possible rather than arranging for junior Ministers to stand in or for the permanent representatives to deputise. The Specialist Agencies need to be staffed by well qualified officials from national defence ministries and from NATO often on secondment, not permanent assignment, rather than by officials retired from other posts with only superannuation ahead. The Assembly needs ambitious well-qualified clerks to staff its committees. Finally, the Members of Parliament serving on WEU should view the Assembly as an opportunity for career development and invaluable foreign affairs training rather than merely as an agreeable sinecure in Paris at the conclusion of an arduous political career.

The collective security and equipment procurement arrangements which underpin Britain's national defence clearly demand a transnational approach to British defence policy formulation. What constitutes the best institutional forum required for this purpose will become increasingly discussed. The European Parliament will have its advocates, mainly out of wishful thinking on the part of those who hope that the European Economic Community will acquire an agreed defence dimension to add to its responsibilities. By treaty it is not officially competent to possess such a dimension nor does its disparate membership, ranging from radical Greece and neutral Eire to Nordic Denmark and Socialist Spain, render it able to fulfil an effective security role. The unsatisfactory experience of the European Community in seeking to agree anti-terrorist policies has certainly not been propitious.

Attempts will be made, primarily by seeking through the European Parliament to agree industrial policies in the defence equipment sector, to arrogate to the Community a defence role, but European public opinion has little respect for the European Parliament and appears wholly unmoved by its deliberations. Another misguided initiative seeking to focus political and public opinion more clearly on the European dimension to national defence policy might be to propose the colocation of all the component parts of WEU at Brussels, supposedly to be closer to the heart of the EEC and more importantly to NATO Headquarters. WEU has very little common ground with the EEC and as for the relationship with NATO, it could well prove difficult since WEU might all too easily be dominated by NATO and lose its identity in the process.

Popular Support for Defence

Finally, defence in a democracy depends on the support of the people in peacetime and not just in emergency or war. It requires the support of the population for whatever armaments, including nuclear weapons, may be required to deter aggression and a sense of popular identification with those who have to bear arms in the cause of national defence. This is easier to achieve if there is substantial popular contact with the Services. However, the reduction in strength of the Armed Forces over the years, the lack of National Service and the low numbers in the Volunteer Reserves have all tended to divorce the Services from the population as a whole. This must be reversed.

The disbandment or amalgamation of some proud regiments with fine historical and local recruiting traditions, has contributed in the past to the distancing of Britain's servicemen from the rest of the community. Regimental ties are one of the greatest strengths of the British Army and officer recruitment has to some extent suffered from the fact that regimental traditions are less strong and family loyalties to the profession of arms are diminishing. There are other social factors at work including greater materialism and a declining sense of service.

The Service Academies

The Armed Forces do not exert themselves adequately to restore a more intense sense of service and personal commitment, most importantly on the part of holders of permanent commissions. The Services have incomparable facilities for training and, to their credit, they place great emphasis on personal development throughout an officer's career. Nevertheless, financial stringency has led to unfortunate economies in professional military education.

The three Service Academies of Dartmouth, Sandhurst and Cranwell, which formerly offered prolonged vocational education for either two or three years, depending upon the Service in question, for cadet entrants from school now run much shorter courses. Whereas these Academies used to prepare a carefully selected elite for the rigours and challenges of a full career commission, today they are more comprehensive in their intake of junior officers for training. That in itself is not regrettable. There are worthwhile economies in concentrating at the Service Academies initial officer training previously conducted at officer cadet training units.

However, no one can pretend that the twenty-eight week standard military course at the Royal Military Academy Sandhurst or the eighteen weeks of basic officer training at the Royal Air Force College, Cranwell can compare in range or scope with the two and three year courses of military education at Sandhurst and Cranwell, respectively, in the 1950s and 1960s. The course for non-graduate career entrants to the Britannia Royal Naval College, Dartmouth has been truncated, although not so badly as the courses at Sandhurst and Cranwell. A rapid turnover of new entrants has been substituted for the traditional objective of a lengthy inculcation of the necessarily special values and qualities required of those officers who are worthy of a full career commission.

It has been the experience of nations with the proudest military traditions and record of success in war, that a small cadre of intensely dedicated full career officers merit military education in depth in the earliest formative years. The rigours and discipline of the profession of arms are unnatural; personal dedication and selfless service demand special inculcation. These qualities are best brought out over a period of years in a Service Academy. Once acquired, they run very deep and bind tightly in a special bond of loyalty, trust and understanding those who have spent years of military education together as officer cadets, a fact which can prove invaluable in posts of higher responsibility later on.

Leadership qualities cannot be brought out adequately by a high intensity syllabus of a few weeks. In service training, throughout an officer's career, admirable and necessary as it is, must be less formative than the intense shared experience of a long course at Dartmouth, Sandhurst or Cranwell. Professional military education in the widest sense is inadequate at the Academies today. The science of war, military history, the traditions of the Services, basic academic study, drill, science, mathematics, physical education and modern languages, all these essential elements in the instruction and development of a career officer are treated far too cursorily. The search for cost savings and for an economic return on investment through an early entry into operational service of the new officer have become the dominating influences in this important aspect of manpower policy.

The new short courses at the Service Academies have evolved not merely to save money. Quite rightly the Armed Forces have been steadily increasing their intake of graduates from the Universities and Polytechnics. The profession of arms becomes more intellectually challenging and technically demanding with the passage of time. Growing numbers of school-leavers aspire to go to university as a natural progression after school, leaving their ultimate choice of career to graduation time or shortly before. A University degree is regarded by many young people if not as their right then at least as an insurance policy for the future and a ticket (even if no guarantee) to secure employment.

These facts were recognised in the report on Officer Education by Professor Sir Michael Howard and Sir Cyril English commissioned by the then Secretary of State for Defence in 1966. Since that time the Armed Forces have if anything overstressed the appropriateness of a university education to their officer requirements, particularly the Royal Air Force which for over ten years has replaced the Trenchardian model of cadet entry into the Royal Air Force College, Cranwell with the Graduate Entry Scheme.

No one has summarised better the objectives of professional military education than Sir Michael Howard himself in a seminar to the Royal United Services Institute for Defence Studies fifteen years ago.

> *"What I have to say now consists basically of a summary of what we then told the Secretary of State. We broke down the requirement for the education of officers into three parts, like Gaul – the need for character formation and character training to turn the boy into a man and the man into a leader; the need for technical training to enable him to handle the growing complexity of technological tools which will be at his disposal during his career; and, third, and not least, the intellectual and moral education of the officer as a young man as a whole, the stretching of his mind. We felt that this last aspect was particularly important in the latter half of the 20th century because of three things: first, because of the horrifying responsibilities of the armed forces in an age of nuclear weapons; secondly, because of the political implications of the use of armed force at almost every level. (At this stage the implications were still international, but the possibility of their becoming something less than international was already apparent.) The third aspect, which worried me most and still does, was that of the possible isolation of the armed forces in a civilian community as the experience of the last war gets further and further away, with all the problems they were likely to face as a result."*[1]

These objectives are equally valid, not more so today.

The Recommendations of the Howard/English Report as it became known also set in perspective the relevance of a university education as a preparation for a career in the Armed Services.:

> *"But there seem to me to be three drawbacks to university education for officers. First, it is difficult to find in the universities in this country today studies wholly appropriate to the requirements of the officer concerned. I do not say that they do not exist, but I do not think that anywhere they cover the whole field which I have outlined. Secondly, the qualifications for becoming an officer are quite properly not necessarily those which are looked for for entry into a university. There is a considerable overlap, but they are not identical, and there are and will continue to be many splendid young men whom the armed forces would be delighted to get as officers but who, for good or bad reasons, the universities do not consider qualified to undertake their courses.*

Since there will thus be a substantial number of young officers who cannot get into universities, the danger arises that you might get a two-tier military structure, divided into the 'fliers' who have been to universities and therefore seem obviously destined for higher promotion, and those who have not, and who therefore may feel that they are second class citizens throughout their career. This does not arise when you have a subtantial cadre of officers educated in the great military colleges, Sandhurst, Cranwell, Dartmouth – providing the bulk of your officer material into which your university intake and your short-service intake can be geared, amalgamated and, in the contemporary jargon, 'socialised'."[2]

In the United States the problem of providing appropriate military education has been tackled head on by making the three Service Academies of Annapolis, Colorado Springs and West Point degree awarding institutions. At the same time the Armed Forces take graduate entrants for career commissions from the Universities after service in the University Reserve Officer Training Corps. In this manner none of the professionalism of the Academies is lost, indeed they have been admirably adapted to developing the exceptional intellectual and personal qualities required of career officers to-day.

To some extent the degree awarding courses for engineering officers at the Royal Military College of Science at Shrivenham at the Royal Naval Engineering College at Manadon have particular merit. However they are for technical specialists only and need to be reinforced by more character training and a broader educational curriculum of military history and the humanities.

The Need for a Joint Service Cadet College

It is this synthesis of broad military education and the development of exceptional personal qualities which is so difficult to achieve. The Howard/English Report recommended that officer entrants of all three Services should do a year of academic study together in a single tri-Service college after a year in their respective single-Service cadet colleges learning to be soldiers, sailors and airmen.

The concept was good but would be much better the other way round. Entry to the tri-Service Cadet College, preferably located at the Royal Naval College, Greenwich, should be directly from school. This would help those whose personal qualities were promising but who lacked the level of education needed to enable them to cope with the demands of professional Service instruction today.

Those officer cadets with a science background would benefit from the instruction in language, logic, thinking and writing, from the humanities generally and from strategic studies. Officer cadets with a humanities background would benefit from instruction in mathematics and physics, from a study of scientific thought and method, engineering principles and technology. Both categories would recieve joint courses in military history, physical training and drill and in the traditions of the Services. All this would be done in an impressive setting close to London, in the public eye, but above all in a strict, disciplined environment. Those entrants who lacked the necessary application and character would be eliminated from what the French rightly call "formation", not simply training. Those who were successful would progress to Dartmouth, Sandhurst and Cranwell where they would be joined by their graduate entry counterparts for in-depth single-Service training.

Having graduated from Dartmouth, Sandhurst, and Cranwell the future officer must know that he has constant opportunities for self improvement and courses of instruction. There should be opportunities for a degree in military science within the Armed Forces themselves, as proposed by H.R.H. the Duke of Edinburgh. However early retirement in favour of service in the Reserves should be made more acceptable, and regarded as a perfectly normal career option. The Reserve Forces lack good officers at present and would benefit greatly from more ex-regulars. The new pattern of officer education would be more broadly based and with a wider academic content. The gap between the graduate and non-graduate entrant would be smaller and inter-service co-operation learned at the earliest stage.

Restoring the Prestige of the Profession of Arms

Understandably something has to be done to restore the prestige of the profession of arms. There must be more contact between the civil and military communities in Britain. Conscription would help but it is not the whole answer to the need to achieve more general public awareness of the necessity for strong national defences. Strong volunteer Reserves are a positive factor as is a vigorous, healthy defence industrial base. Industry, particularly defence equipment companies, should actively recruit more former Regulars and serving Volunteer Reservists.

The effective involvement of the resources of a nation for its own defence requires a total strategy taking into account such factors as shipping, air transport, industrial potential, skill indentification, training and mobilisation plus an almost sociological approach to secure public backing and enthusiastic support for the security policies of Government. The Armed Forces have a role to play in this process, especially if National Service could be reintroduced, the Reserves of all three Services strengthened, and the quality of education and training of all those within the Services enhanced.

CHAPTER V

Manpower. The Thin Red Line

BRITAIN's Thin Red Line[1] is getting thinner. Soon it will break. In the past twenty years the strength of her armed forces has declined by no less than twenty-three per cent from 418,400 to 323,500. In France over the same period the reduction was only five point six per cent.

With the exception of Iceland and Luxembourg, Britain is the only NATO European country which does not have military national service. Her defence manpower policy of small, professional, long service volunteers aims to achieve quality rather than quantity. In consequence, her armed forces are amongst the highest trained, most efficient and best disciplined in the Western Alliance. Their performance in the South Atlantic in 1982 and in Ulster over a much longer period and in the most exacting circumstances is proof of this assessment.

But it is an extremely expensive policy and vulnerable to adverse trends in the national economy, especially inflation. For professional, and often highly qualified and technically proficient, people rates of pay have to compete with those on offer in civil life, and the accompanying allowances and benefits, which include housing, family welfare services and children's education, add substantially to the costs of armed forces manpower. The index-linked pensions paid to long service regulars on retirement are also an item in personnel costs; in 1986–87 there were some 223,000 service pensioners and at £986 million the annual cost of their pensions represented five per cent of the defence budget.

It is also an uneconomical and in some ways an extravagant policy, as the experience of the last decade shows. If, in its wish to economise on defence spending, the Government allows forces' pay rates to fall below what is perceived to be an acceptable level, as it had done by 1978, then the outflow of officers and men who leave before the expiry of their engagement, either by request for premature release or by exercise of their right to leave at an option point, increases and large pay rises have to be awarded to halt this trend.

The total pay bill then mounts to a level which the defence budget is unable to support, particularly if this coincides with a period of substantial rises in the costs of new weapons and equipment, and manpower strengths have to be reduced. Since commitments remain unaltered, signs of overstretch begin to appear, the conditions of service deteriorate and the rate of voluntary outflow starts to rise again to create an overall reduction in manpower even larger than that which it is desired to achieve to contain the pay bill. So real increases in pay have to be awarded once again and the equipment budget comes under renewed pressure. Such a situation had been reached by the spring of 1986 and was the main cause of an average effective pay increase for the armed forces of five point six per cent for 1986–87 compared with an annual inflation rate of under three per cent at the time of the award.

Present defence manpower policy is extravagant in its permissive attitude to premature release. For professional forces, whose performance reflects their traditional excellence, training costs are high, particularly for the engineering, electronics and technical branches, and above all for aircrew. Yet no restrictions on the early release of these highly trained people are imposed. In a Commons debate on the Royal Air Force in February 1986 an Opposition defence spokesman claimed that in the current year no less than 236 pilots and 115 navigators would leave before completion of their engagements compared with the 161 pilots and fifty-three navigators who would graduate from flying training schools. Pointing out that it costs £2.87 million to train a fast jet pilot and £1 million to train a navigator, he estimated that it had cost almost £1 billion to train the pilots and navigators who were leaving early and would need another £1 billion to replace them, even if they could be found from the recruiting process.

> *"They are literally worth their weight in gold. Many of them are leaving to take up better paid jobs with civil airlines . . . We must also question whether civilian airlines, if they are taking aircrew who are retiring prematurely, should not make some contribution to training the officers. British Airways did away with its pilot training school some time ago."*[2]

It is arguable too that the Royal Air Force ought, on economic grounds alone, to maintain reserve flying units to absorb aircrew who leave after short service engagements.

Whether the defence budget is growing or falling in real terms the experience of 1979–86 shows that the proportion of Gross Domestic Product which a Conservative government is prepared to allocate to national security will not support armed forces of more than 315,000–320,000 under the present expensive manpower policy without unacceptable damage to the equipment budget. Nor in the long term would a Labour government be disposed to maintain larger forces despite its promises of support for the conventional arms after the proposed scrapping of Trident. Without new policies amongst the NATO allies Britain will continue to have the lowest proportion of its population in the armed forces with the exeption of Canada and Luxembourg. As the total strength of the forces falls, the claim that quality makes up for the decreasing quantity is correspondingly weakened.

But what sized armed forces does Britain actually need as the twenty-first century approaches? Foreign and strategic policy, national security needs, the contribution to the collective security provided by NATO, the most appropriate "threat scenario", and, last but by no means least, domestic and social policies have to be considered in preparing a worthwhile answer to this question. That radical changes in many of these areas are long overdue must be apparent already.

The obsessive maintenance of the strategic status quo has to be broken and the policy of the four Cs (See page 16) changed fundamentally to blend more realistically with national defence needs and the country's contribution to NATO's collective security system. Britain's new defence and strategic policy should be based on the circumstances of the twenty-first century rather than on those of the mid-fifties in which it has been stuck for too long. The principles on which the policy ought to be prepared can already be discerned. They will largely determine the future pattern of armed forces manpower.

It is the duty of a government to provide for the defence of the realm and the fact that "defence begins at home" should be engraved on the hearts of all those who aspire to participate in the policy-making process. Militarily, the provision of a comprehensive, all-round, forward and in-depth defence system for the United Kingdom, much of which would by its very nature represent the country's contribution to NATO's defence plans, must be the first requirement, and it should be supported to a far greater degree than is the case today by standing arrangements – the efficacy of which would be regularly exercised – to mobilise rapidly the nation's reserves (particularly of skilled manpower, such as aircraft pilots and seafarers) and to take up from trade for military use the vital civil assets such as aircraft, helicopters, shipping and road transport without which resistance could not be sustained for more than a brief period.

Flexibility and mobility should be the hallmarks of Britain's armed forces of the future, as capable of providing a rapid deployment force for operations outside the NATO area in the defence of national or allied interests as of assisting in the defence of that area by land, sea or in the air. These are the traditional military tasks of deterrence against acts of war which will have to be carried out for the foreseeable future and which would become even more important in the event of a super-power agreement on the reduction of nuclear arsenals.

However, there is another aspect to the defence of the realm equation. In Europe politicians can justifiably claim that NATO's combination of nuclear and conventional deterrent forces has kept the peace for forty years, but under this umbrella all manner of low intensity threats to national security and well-being have intensified and proliferated, notably, of course, the politically motivated resort to terrorism and violence. Traditionally, the countering of such threats has been the responsibility of the civil police, but from time to time they have had to call for assistance from specialist military forces such as Britain's Special Air Service Regiment (SAS), and the trend of international terrorist activity seems likely to make such calls more frequent.

In the United Kingdom the experience of Ulster, where the separation of the roles of the police and the military has barely succeeded in containing the level of such activity, let alone in defeating it, shows that a more integrated civil-military effort is necessary, however politically distasteful, if a well-planned terrorist campaign is to be defeated. A new defence policy should take account of the whole range of low intensity threats to national security which now beset the western nations, terrorism, drugs, illegal immigration, subversion, to mention only the most serious and should seek to promote greater public involvement in the fight against them.

A defence and strategic policy such as has been described will require rather larger numbers of standing armed forces than the 320,000 or so highly trained regulars which is all that the likely future level of British defence spending will be able to afford, and a substantial increase in the numbers of trained reservists available for mobilisation at short notice. Basically, a smaller core of expensive long service professionals must be augmented by larger numbers of men and women engaged for a shorter term and ineligible for the benefits, allowances and pensions of the regulars. A short engagement of this nature should be followed by a statutory commitment to enlistment in the reserves and to an annual period of training for a given number of years.

It will by now be apparent that the reintroduction of military national service in Britain would meet all the manpower objectives of the defence and strategic policy which the country needs to adapt to the twenty-first century. Whatever course is pursued in the matter of military manpower, it has to be stressed that smaller armed forces are no longer an available option for a British government seeking yet more economies in its defence budget. Such further diminution of military capability would remove Britain from the first division of West European powers, a relegation which the British people would not wish to see despite some appearances to the contrary, and one which would seriously weaken the NATO Alliance at a time when strength and unity are needed as never before to combat the many diverse influences aiming to divide it.

The Reserve Forces

Britain's manpower policy for her regular forces is unique in Western Europe. The organisation of her reserve forces is similarly unique. National service as practised on the continent of Europe provides a steady flow of men who are transferred to the reserves for a limited time on completion of their call-up period. Britain however relies on a combination of former members of the regular forces with a liability for reserve service and of volunteers from civilian life who offer their services for a specified number of days training each year.

With budgetary restraints limiting both the size and the equipment of the reserves (in 1986–87 they received a paltry 1.9 per cent of the defence budget) Britain has the smallest proportion of the population enrolled in the reserves of any NATO country including the USA.

TABLE 5.1
BRITAIN'S RESERVE FORCES
1986

	(Thousands)
Royal Navy	
Regular Reserves	23.9
Volunteer Reserves and Auxiliary Forces	5.2
Royal Marines	
Regular Reserves	2.3
Volunteer Reserves and Auxiliary Forces	1.1
Army	
Regular Reserves	152.7
Territorial Army	76.1
Ulster Defence Regiment	6.5
Home Service Force	2.9
Royal Air Force	
Regular Reserves	30.9
Volunteer Reserves and Auxiliary Forces	1.3
TOTALS	
Regular Reserves	209.7
Volunteer Reserves and Auxiliary Forces	93.1

At first sight the numbers of Britain's regular reserves appear reassuring but the reality behind them is hardly comforting. Their legally binding liability to 15 days per year annual training is never enforced owing to lack of employment protection legislation (a typical example of the lack of interdepartmental co-operation which bedevils the adoption of sensible defence manpower policies) and reluctance to prosecute those reservists who fail to attend. As the years go by the regular reserves therefore cease to be properly trained in modern weapons or new fighting methods.

Aware of these shortcomings, the Government introduced a voluntary call-out scheme in 1985 to give Regular Army reservists a week's refresher training in the third year after their discharge from the colours. The initial response was disappointing, but in 1986, encouraged by a tax-free training bounty of £115, fifty per cent of those eligible volunteered and reported for this training. By contrast, the volunteer reserve forces make up with enthusiasm what they lack in numbers. Thanks to their annual training commitment, they could be a more useful reinforcement of the nation's defences on mobilisation than their ex-regular counterparts.

The present composition of Britain's reserve forces is unbalanced, too supportive of the outmoded "single scenario" NATO strategy which successive governments have espoused for so long, and too neglectful of the needs of home defence. In particular, the lack of a reserve of combat aircraft and of pilots to man them to augment the front-line strength of the Royal Air Force is a serious flaw in the whole reserve organisation.

Army regular reservists and the volunteer Territorial Army (TA) comprise seventy-three per cent of the country's reserves. But unlike the other three volunteer reserve forces (Royal Naval Reserve, Royal Auxiliary Air Force and Royal Air Force Volunteer Reserve), the Territorial Army includes all arms and specialisations of the British Army of which, on mobilisation, it would form almost one quarter. Should this occur, fifty per cent of both the TA and the Army regular reserves would be despatched to West Germany to treble the size of the Army of the Rhine. The remainder would be available for home defence.

No warships are now kept in reserve ready to be manned by naval reservists in an emergency. The wartime tasks of the navy's volunteer reserves (the RNR) are to augment the country's none too plentiful mine warfare forces by manning the twelve new fleet minesweepers recently allocated to them and, with older volunteers, to form the nucleus of a naval control of shipping organisation to prepare for a convoy system. Here at least is a welcome – if modest-indication that the "short war" philosophy is not universally prevalent.

The complete lack of any form of reserve air force has already been remarked upon. Over the years, despite much criticism from informed observers of the defence scene (and not least from one of the authors of this work), the Royal Air Force has consistently opposed the creation of such a force and the miniscule volunteer element of its reserves is trained for various ground tasks of a specialist variety and to augment the airfield defence role of the RAF Regiment. However, it must be recorded that in 1986 a thin ray of light appeared to relieve this discouraging scene. Discussing the RAF's Air Transport Force (ATF), the Defence White Paper disclosed somewhat coyly that:

> *"A two-year trial of a RAF Volunteer Reserve crew flying on VC10s from Brize Norton is just beginning, the first time the RAFVR has provided aircrew for a front-line aircraft for over 20 years."*[3]

This candid admission encapsulates a most welcome development.

Since 1979 the Conservative Government has initiated a number of improvements to Britain's reserve forces. From a strength of 59,000 in 1979 the Territorial Army is to be increased in size to a target of 86,000 by 1990. This may prove to be an optimistic figure for by 1986 turnover in some TA units was already running at unacceptably high levels (thirty per cent in some cases), foreshadowing future problems with further recruitment. A Home Service Force has been formed for the defence of key installations in war with an initial target recruitment of 7,000 older reservists with three years service experience. Ministers were at last beginning to appreciate the shortcomings of the home defence organisation to which Sir John Nott had drawn attention back in 1981.

The supply of new minesweepers to the Royal Naval Reserve (RNR) has already been mentioned. But plans to make a substantial and long overdue increase in the size of this force seem to have been abandoned. In November 1984 the Government announced that it was aiming to increase the planned strength of the RNR by well over forty per cent over the next few years from around 5,400 to 7,800[4], yet by 1986 its strength had actually fallen to 5,200.

TABLE 5.2
British Army. 1986
Annual Costs of Regular and Reserve Soldiers

Soldier in Regular Forces	*£12,800*
Soldier in Territorial Army	*£2,800*
Soldier in Home Service Force	*£770*

The regular forces view these increases in the volunteer reserves with mixed feelings. Whilst admitting that such reserves offer value for money, senior officers tend nevertheless to resent increased spending on them when their own budgets are under pressure, as they almost continually are. Fears that the professionalism and élitism which have become the hallmarks of the regular forces may be undermined and diluted by larger reserves are also in evidence. In February 1985, in a lecture at the Royal United Services Institute for Defence Studies in London, the Inspector General of the Territorial Army claimed that to expand the TA beyond the target of 86,000 would impose "a great and unacceptable burden on the regulars who train and support them".

> *"If we go beyond that limit we may get numbers on the cheap, but it won't be defence. It all boils down, therefore, to a judgment on the best balance between numbers and quality, by which I really mean combat readiness."*[5]

If typical of the Army establishment, this astonishing view from a senior officer, whose main responsibility was to encourage the TA and its concept of voluntary part-time service, hardly augurs well for the degree of support that will be forthcoming for any extension of this concept which new defence manpower policies may require.

Britain needs a larger proportion of her citizens to be enrolled in or associated with her reserve forces. The present combination of ex-regular and volunteer reserves will not provide it nor will the likely future level of defence spending pay for such an expansion or for the bigger stockpiles of weapons and equipment which more reservists would require without unacceptable cuts in other sectors of the defence budget.

Just as with the regular forces, a new concept is needed for the reserves which will draw on the latent skills, abilities and enthusiasms of the people as a whole to enhance and expand the defences of the country against the many and varied threats which it will face in the future from terrorism to nuclear bombardment. Such a concept should take account of the social and economic problems which afflict the nation today and seem likely to continue to do so, and should be designed to provide a significant contribution towards their solution, notably in reducing youth unemployment and in improving the supply of skilled and motivated manpower.

Almost twenty years ago, discussing the review of the Army reserves which the Labour Government of the day was about to carry out, a respected and far-sighted defence correspondent suggested how the reviewers should approach their task. His ideas are even more relevant today:

> *"The most important reserve, and the most difficult of all these to reproduce in a hurry is trained manpower. But it is the armed forces training machine which, in its broadest sense, now has most to offer for the general economic and social benefit of the whole country. We should take advantage of this to develop a reserve military capacity, by using the service training machine to turn out trained men who would have a reservist status for some years after their training, but who would spend no other full time with the colours."*[6]

Here too lie the seeds of an answer to the question of how to pay for an increase in Britain's reserve forces. From 1987–88 some 395,000 young people will enrol in the enlarged two-year Youth Training Scheme (YTS) at an annual cost of £790 million. Whilst the defence budget is being reduced in real terms to contain the overall level of government expenditure, that of the employment department will be increased to £3.741 billion in 1987–88 to pay for this scheme and other measures to help both the young and the long-term unemployed.

It ought now to be within the capabilities of an imaginative and constructive government, free of narrow inter-departmental jealousies, to realise that a re-allocation of some of these extra financial resources from Employment to Defence would achieve two highly desirable objectives. Reserve forces would be increased, their capabilities improved, and at the same time youth training would benefit and the skills and abilities which young people could offer in their search for work greatly expanded. Precisely the same desirable consequences would flow from a reintroduction of military national service which in the broadest interests of the country could be financed in the same way.

A Return to Military National Service

> *"Conscription is the one serious demonstration of a country's desire to enlist all its citizens in the defence of their society; and here it is ignored."*[7]

To relinquish National Service in the conditions of the early 1960s was a politically appealing policy (see page 5) with desirable economic and social consequences and one which would at that time neither prejudice the needs of national security nor cause military commitments to be abandoned. A quarter of a century later, its reintroduction, for very different reasons to those given at the time in support of its cessation, is becoming the subject of serious discussion. Why is this so?

Britain needs a new policy for its armed forces manpower and its reserves. Both are now too small. National Service would produce larger standing forces and a steady flow of reserves. To the extent tthat British forces will continue to be assigned to NATO commands in war, conscription would make a modest contribution to the raising of the nuclear threshold in Europe, a point of greater political than military significance in view of the defence policy of the official opposition party in Britain.

Indeed, unless the Labour Party is prepared to transform Britain into a defenceless neutral at the mercy of any major aggressor, its non-nuclear defence policy must logically require a major increase in conventional defence capabilities including larger forces and reserves. Even after the net savings which would accrue from the cancellation of the Trident programme, conscripts would be the only form of manpower in which any government, let alone a Labour one, could afford to effect increases of any meaningful size.

It is however towards the broader social and moral benefits to the state of the nation arising from national service that a great deal of the discussion is directed, especially the questions of youth training and youth employment. In this respect military service is perceived as an increasingly necessary antidote to the absence of discipline and of a sense of social duty and responsibility in the upbringing of all too many young people.

As a Conservative MP explained in a Commons debate on the Royal Air Force in February 1986:

> *"We also rightly recognise the role that the armed forces can play in educating, in the broadest sense, our young people – giving them skills, training, and experience of work away from home in an ordered and structured environment, having to defer to authority and learning social behaviour and patterns of social responsibility which will be of great value to them in later life."*[8]

This view echoes the opinion of a former National Serviceman given in a letter to the Imperial War Museum on the opening of its National Service Exhibition in September 1986:

> *"I can only endorse comments from many other National Servicemen that what at first seemed to be two years waste of time living on inferior wages in sometimes poor accommodation and very often inadequate food turned out to be an experience that was unforgettable in the comradeship and understanding that was formed between young men in the same situation from all walks of life."*[9]

By its nature, National Service increases public awareness of the need to defend the realm and provides the means for involvement in that defence. However, in the world of today its scope should be widened to include the campaign against the whole range of what – for want of a better phrase – can be described as low intensity threats to a country's stability and security and to the lives of its inhabitants which feature increasingly in their lives (see page 64). For this reason Britain should follow the example of France and include service in the police in any new policy of conscription for national service.

TABLE 5.3
FRANCE 1986
Employment of Conscripts

Army	182,622
Air Force	36,454
Navy	18,569
Gendarmerie	8,571
Inter-Service Central Staffs	2,106
	248,322

That political, social, and administrative as well as budgetary problems would arise in the process of reintroducing National Service into the Britian of the eighties is undeniable, but no government which has a genuine desire to revive the patriotism and restore the spirit of the nation should shrink from tackling them. Mr. Kinnock should remind his party that forty years ago, in October 1946, the Labour Cabinet of Clement Attlee agreed that in the Welfare State which they were then constructing there was an obligation on all citizens to undertake National Service.[10]

Two topical matters can be mentioned here. The decline in educational standards which has taken place during the past twenty years, especially the lack of discipline and authority in the teaching process, would undoubtedly cause problems, but with the improvements in these areas which in the national interest any future government must soon introduce, these difficulties should be surmountable. Bearing in mind that over a two-year period to 1986 of the 9,000 applicants for places under the Armed Services Youth Training Scheme (ASYTS) only 2,700 reached the standards for acceptance that the Services considered necessary, it must be assumed that a considerable number of young men presenting themselves for call-up today would lack the mental and physical qualities of the generation of twenty-five years ago.[11]

This assumption is borne out by a warning from the Minister responsible for higher education of the danger of Britain becoming a "remedial society" with forty per cent of youngsters on the Youth Training Scheme (YTS) having to be given remedial teaching in writing, reading and counting after ten years of full-time education.[12]

No doubt both white and coloured young people would be included in this category requiring yet more elementary education. But for the latter National Service could bring other benefits of a social nature. To help to defend the country would give the ethnic minorities a stronger sense of belonging to the community through active participation in a really worthwhile national object. The rigours of military discipline constitute a practical and unifying exercise in community relations. A more committed and imaginative approach to the problems of assimilation of the ethnic minorities is long overdue. National Service would provide it.

The administrative problems associated with any return to conscription in Britain have been outlined elsewhere as have the major decisions which the Government would have to take in order to establish a sensible and workable system which the nation would understand and accept.[13] From the point of view of defence and strategic policy the most important of these would be the proportions of the manpower of each service which would be provided by regular long service professionals and by National Servicemen respectively. Herein lie issues very sensitive to professional pride which can instantly arouse hidden fears within the regular forces, especially in the Army, which must necessarily bear the brunt of the burden of training conscripts.

It would be the duty of ministers to allay these fears which are not solely concerned with the dilution of professional excellence, and to rouse the enthusiasm of the forces to play what would be a leading part in a vital national task. As a Conservative MP pointed out in a Commons debate on the Army in January 1986:

> *"Why is it that many of us, myself included, have only recently become converts to this idea? (National Service) I suspect that it is because politicians have swallowed the quite understandable line of the military establishment that it would be a retrograde step, not to mention sheer hard work, to go back to a system which was abandoned in the 1960s. There is a great deal of institutional inertia in the military establishments."*[14]

The Cost

By 1986 the creaking hull of the British defence budget had become rudderless, drifting helplessly between the Scylla of still rising costs for manpower and conventional arms (a danger dominated by the gigantic costs of the Nimrod AEW disaster) and the Charybdis of the Trident programme. The steering engine provided by an annual increase in the budget in rcal terms, which has imparted some sense of direction from 1979 to 1985, had been removed by the Government's fit of pre-election nerves in switching its financial priorities from weapons to welfare as so many of its predecessors had done in the post-war years.

With such a financially bleak outlook, the prospects for a reintroduction of National Service look dim indeed. Conscription would be an expensive step even though once the capital costs of new barracks, training facilities, and equipment had been met, it would provide the source of less expensive manpower and the flow of reserves which the country needs to prevent the size of its forces falling to unacceptable levels.

However, this would be to look at the problem within the narrow parameters of the defence budget and to consider the reintroduction of National Service purely as a defence policy item. This would be entirely the wrong approach to a matter of the greatest national importance affecting, as it would, the whole thrust of government policy for the administration of the country and embracing the economy, employment, education and youth training as well as national security. National Service could not be reintroduced without breaking down the rigidities of departmental budgets and responsibilities which have so often bedevilled the conduct of the present British Government's business. The Westland affair was a classic example of this phenomenon.

There is an urgent need to re-examine the whole question of defence spending, not solely in terms of the cost of military capabilities needed for national security in all its aspects, but with a much broader consideration of the national interest in mind. In the latter half of the 1980s this means a policy for both defence manpower and procurement where the decisions taken by defence ministers will combine military needs with an alleviation of the over-riding national problems of unemployment, the rundown of the country's manufacturing base and its maritime assets, and the training of youth.

The naval building programme provides a useful example of what is in mind. In February 1986 in a Commons debate on the Royal Navy, the Government had announced its intention to order the second of the new Type 23 frigates from Swan Hunter Shipbuilders, subject to agreement on price.[15] By early June, no more had been heard of new frigate orders and Swan Hunter announced over 800 redundancies with the threat of more to follow if the Government did not fulfil its promised orders. The Swan Hunter frigate order was finally announced on July 15th. Yet, if the defence budget was under such day-to-day strain as this incident would seem to imply, could not funds approximating to the costs of redundancy payments and unemployment benefits which would have been incurred by delayed ordering have been transferred to Defence from the Department of Health and Social Security, thus preserving jobs and shipbuilding capacity? The House of Commons Defence Committee took up the point in its Second Report for 1985-86 covering the 1986 Defence Estimates:

> *"Conversely, the real cost to the taxpayer of, say, new frigates at a time of severe recession in the shipbuilding industry is very much less than the 'list price', which takes no account of saved unemployment benefit and expenditure on special unemployment measures, to say nothing of the maintenance of strategic industrial facilities. We recognise the difficulties of determining 'non-defence' costs. Where these can be determined, however, we think it unreasonable that such costs should fall upon the defence budget, particularly at a time of real defence cuts."*[16]

Cross-Channel Comparisons

Britain and France are two West European nations with broadly similar population totals and profiles, particularly in the 18-30 age group from which the overwhelming majority of personnel for national defence has to be drawn (see Table 5.4). A comparison of the pattern of armed forces provided by a blend of a core of professionals backed by conscription on the one hand and by a system of voluntary long-service wholly professional forces on the other is, therefore, instructive. Should Britian switch back from a pattern of all-volunteer engagements to conscription, an annual total of some quarter of a million National Servicemen undergoing training or serving in the forces would seem to be a not unrealistic planning figure. If the principle of extending national service to the police and to other non-military organisations engaged in the fight against low-intensity threats to society is accepted, then a pattern of employment for conscripts can be drawn up.

TABLE 5.4
THE UNITED KINGDOM
Suggested Employment of National Servicemen

Army	160,000
Royal Air Force	40,000
Royal Navy	35,000
Police	12,000
HM Coastguard	1,000
Customs & Excise	1,000
Immigration Service	1,000
	250,000

To maintain a realistic balance between the professional head and the national service body the resulting manpower profile for Britain's armed forces might look like this:

TABLE 5.5
BRITAIN & FRANCE
MILITARY MANPOWER 1986

	BRITAIN		FRANCE	
Population		56,132,000		55,502,000
Men 18–30		5,737,000		5,609,000
Women 18–30		5,511,000		5,432,000
Total Regular Forces	323,500		232,610	
of which:				
Male		307,400		219,010
Female		16,100		13,600
Total Conscripts	–		239,751	
Total Armed Forces		323,500		472,361
Total Defence Civilians		203,700		141,853
Forces				
Army	162,100		296,480	
of which:				
Male Regulars		155,500		107,608
Female ,,		6,600		6,250
Conscripts				182,622
Navy	60,700		66,345	
of which:				
Male Regulars		(a) 57,200		46,276
Female ,,		3,500		1,500
Conscripts		–		18,569
Air Force	93,100		95,978	
of which:				
Male Regulars		87,100		53,674
Female ,,		6,000		5,850
Conscripts		–		36,454
Marines	7,600		–	
Inter-Service Central	–			
Staffs			13,558	
of which:				
Regulars				11,452
Conscripts				2,106
Reserves				
Army		(b) 238,200		305,000
Navy		29,100		28,000
Air Force		32,200		58,000
Marines		3,400		–
Total Reserves	302,900		391,000	

(Sources: *SDE 1986 Cmnd 9763 – II.* "*The Military Balance 1986–7*" and French Government publications)
Notes: (a) Excludes 7,600 Royal Marines
(b) Includes 6,500 Ulster Defence Regiment

TABLE 5.6
NATIONAL SERVICE
A Possible Manpower Profile

Royal Navy & Royal Marines	90,000	
Regulars		55,000
Nat. Servicemen		35,000
Army	280,000	
Regulars		120,000
Nat. Servicemen		160,000
Royal Air Force	100,000	
Regulars		60,000
Nat. Servicemen		40,000

An Alternative Solution

Should political temerity, administrative inertia and financial restraints continue to combine successfully against the reintroduction of National Service in Britain, there is one other way in which a smaller cadre of regular professional forces could be combined with others engaged for a shorter term and eligible only for the basic pay of their rank or rating.

This would be by a major expansion of the volunteer reserve forces and by their transformation into part-time members of the armed forces who, instead of merely attending for a specified number of days training and a two weeks annual camp as at present, would be required, after an initial training, to perform an annual period of service with their ship, unit or squadron of several weeks at least. The concept of such a scheme was outlined by the authors elsewhere[17] and was put forward in more detail in the "Defence Policy" study of the Omega Report published by the Adam Smith Institute in 1983[18] in which they also participated.

Administratively cumbersome as it may at first sight appear, a scheme of this nature could well form a part of the forthcoming reorganisation of its industrial, social, employment and fiscal policies which Britain will soon be obliged to undertake to meet the changing pattern of human work and the decline of conventional employment and its culture.[19] Without such a reorganisation, the appallingly heavy national incubus of official "unemployment" whether of youth or of older people will never be satisfactorily cured. As the Omega Defence Report explained:

> *"The aim should be to provide means whereby the people can contribute more widely and actively to the defence of the country as part of the changes in employment which will be introduced. Part time military service on a voluntary basis should be an available option for people when deciding how to make use of greater leisure and more flexible working and career patterns."*[20]

In Britain, the present system of expensive all-professional forces engaged on a long-term career basis and of small volunteer reserve organisations is breaking down. Within the constraints imposed by the likely level of defence spending acceptable to any future government, it will no longer produce standing forces and reserves of the size the country requires for national security and to retain its traditional status as the leading military power in Western Europe. The necessary increases in defence manpower can be achieved either through a system of complusory service or voluntary engagement. But whatever system is adopted, it will be essential to instil a sense of involvement in national defence in all those who serve. Useful training and active employment directly concerned with combating the threats to society and national security at all levels should form the foundations of whatever system is adopted to augment the armed forces of Britain in the twenty-first century.

CHAPTER VI

Defence Technology for Tomorrow

For the United Kingdom, identifying tomorrow's defence technologies, developing them and procuring the resultant weapon systems of the future is a more difficult process than for other European members of NATO. Alone among the European members of the Atlantic Alliance, Britain rejects conscription and must pay the Armed Forces military salaries which are competitive with those available for comparable skills in civilian life. This constrains the defence equipment budget and restricts the amount of money which can be spent on defence research and development. Apart from France, only Britain maintains an independent nuclear deterrent which places special demands on the defence budget. Britain keeps balanced forces of all arms, assigned primarily to NATO but capable of world-wide operation, and this too leads to further exceptional expense.

The multiplicity of special demands on Britain's defence budget makes the achievement of cost effectiveness in weapon procurement essential and the lack of British Service manpower puts a premium on weapon system performance. Furthermore, the cost of acquisition of defence equipment has grown faster historically than the rate of inflation. This relative price effect is a particular problem, especially when defence expenditure is not increasing in real terms. The traditional consensus is that something has to give, that the circle cannot be squared.

Of course political commitments are not necessarily immutable and military strategies can be adapted to accord with budgetary and industrial realities. Some adaptions which have merit in their own right have been expounded forcefully. Other measures can and already are being taken by the Ministry of Defence in pursuit of the Holy Grail of better value for money out of the defence budget. Competitive tendering, international collaboration, NATO standardisation, less "gold plating" of specifications, less adaptation of specifications once issued by the Ministry of Defence, tri-service commonality of logistic support and maintenance, all of these are commonplace already and on the whole, work well to restrain defence expenditure within acceptable limits.

Profligacy in Procurement

Even so the defence equipment procurement process in Britain is far from perfect. On 12 August 1986 the Comptroller and Auditor General, Sir Gordon Downey reported to Parliament the results of an examination by the National Audit Office (NAO) of the Ministry of Defence's response to recurring criticism by the Public Accounts Committee of the House of Commons of deficiencies in the control by the Ministry of Defence (MOD) and their contractors of the development of new equipment.

The National Audit Office found that the Ministry of Defence "*had not succeeded in overcoming the problems of cost escalation and delays. Although MOD continually refine their guidance on control of equipment development and there have been recent major initiatives to introduce improvements, the long development timescale means it will be some years before the efforts are reflected in the overall pattern and results can be fully evaluated.*"[1] The NAO report repeated many of the criticisms of the House of Commons Select Committee on Defence's Report of five years before into the Ministry of Defence's organisation and procurement.

The Select Committee Report quoted the evidence given in a memorandum by Vickers Limited that "*it is difficult to avoid the conclusion that the structure of the MOD is more concerned to avoid procurement errors, and individual responsibility for error, than to succeed in achieving given procurement objectives within the clear constraints of time, cost and specification.*"[2] The Vickers Limited Memorandum went on to recommend that "*a great deal of administrative cost and delay could in our judgement be eliminated from MOD if there were more formal and frequent contact between industry, at the individual company level and the Armed Servies. In this way a more effective perception by each of the other's requirements and problems could be derived, and with it a basis of trust which could only be beneficial for the short and long term.*"[3]

The Select Committee Report confirms this suggestion in its concluding observations. It identifies the breaking down of the customer-contractor relationship between the Ministry of Defence and its industrial suppliers as one of the two broad critical themes which characterise the equipment procurement process in Britain. "*The notion*", the Select Committee concludes, "*that defence planning can proceed by the Services' developing requirements and then searching for an appropriate contractor to meet them has been undermined by the realities of the design and production of modern weapon systems. Over elaborate and unobtainable technical specifications, optimistic cost performance and delivery estimates waste time and resources to a degree which cannot be afforded. It is therefore necessary to draw industry into its projects at the earliest possible stage.*"

Cutting Bureaucracy in the Procurement Executive

To his credit the former Secretary of State for Defence, Michael Heseltine, appreciated the need for a much more commercial approach to equipment procurement on the part of the Ministry of Defence, and early in 1985 he appointed Peter Levene directly from industry with the specific objective of cutting spiralling equipment costs by instituting competitive tendering, a reduction of cost plus contracts and more effective project management. However, Levene's institutional difficulties have proved formidable. The Procurement Executive itself has been subject to criticism in the Omega Report of the Adam Smith Institute to which the authors contributed and by the Chairman of the Select Committee on Trade and Industry, Kenneth Warren.[4] Formed in 1971 as a separate organisation within the Ministry of Defence in accordance with the recommendations of Sir Derek Rayner (previously of Marks and Spencer Limited), the Procurement Executive has been accused of excessive bureaucracy.

To quote the Vickers Memorandum yet again: "the number of hierarchical levels and of cross departmental committees around which MOD procurement decisions are conducted present, in our judgement significant obstacles to sound and timely decision-making. We know of no parallel arrangement within industry which would handle major procurement decisions in such a cumbersome way."[5] The recommendation of the Omega Report on Defence that the individual Services ought to be permitted to procure more directly from industry as they did with notable success during the Falklands War remains valid.

The second broad theme of the Select Committee on Defence, that as the procurement of weapons systems becomes a more complex task, the ability of the Central staffs to monitor the process has to some extent been resolved. Resource management for equipment procurement within the Ministry of Defence as a whole has been improved following Heseltine's reorganisation of the Central Staffs to give them more authority and following his institution of an Office of Management and Budget. Even so, a proliferation of committees persist and authority has to be obtained by contractors from the Procurement Executive for relatively minor system alterations. Conversely, the Procurement Executive imposes on suppliers a plethora of modifications which delay weapon development and make it more costly.

The Comptroller and Auditor General found that the Ministry of Defence overpaid by £938 million on twelve large defence contracts and by £200 million on a further seven which were cancelled. There is no evidence that collaborative programmes have proved more difficult to manage efficiently than national ones. The problem with collaboration is often an initial one of harmonising and agreeing between potential partners, operational requirements and re-equipment timescales. The record on collaborative projects in Europe is good – Alphajet, Jaguar, Transall, Atlantique, Tornado, HOT, MILAN, Gazelle, Puma, Lynx, the Adour and RB199 aero-engines – the list is long and impressive. The only regret is that the Independent European Programme Group which exists to concert weapon procurement between the European members of NATO has no political dimension and no mechanism exists for it to report to the Assembly of Western European Union (which would be ideal) or to any other elected Assembly of Parliamentarians.

Britain's weapon procurement problems are therefore mainly national. However the Comptroller and Auditor General welcomes the initiatives started by Mr. Levene to improve project management saying: "*Because of the long timescales for development, the extent to which the expected benefits are achieved will not be apparent for some years.*"[6]

Rationalising Departmental Responsibility

In spite of all these constructive measures, major crises, like the the Westland or Nimrod AEW affairs can develop unexpectedly, undermining confidence in the competence of the Ministry of Defence and calling into question the efficacy of important sections of Britain's defence industrial base. Both crises merit consideration in some detail, although in the case of the Nimrod AEW affair the dust has not yet settled. It is earnestly to be hoped that crises comparable to these two traumatic episodes are never permitted to occur again. Both controversies were entirely avoidable and the defence issues which precipitated both of them were evident well in advance.[7]

In the case of Westland a lack of forward orders before the production of the EH 101 Anglo-Italian anti-submarine helicopter built up was bound to place great strain on the company's financial resources which were over-stretched in meeting the development costs of the 101. To what extent the Ministry of Defence should be held to blame for the crisis is arguable, since it is debatable whether securing the financial health of an important defence equipment supplier by providing that supplier with orders, which it would otherwise not obtain, is correct policy on the part of the Ministry of Defence.

Is securing a strategically significant but not necessarily crucial part of Britain's defence industrial base the true function of the Ministry of Defence, especially when, as in the case of Westland, the company concerned has a "sponsoring" Government Department? The Department of Trade and Industry is supposedly specifically responsible in the most general sense for the health and welfare of the aerospace industry and so, to a degree it is, since technically, strategically and economically, helicopter manufacture is a significant part of the aircraft industry as a whole.

In the United Kingdom, the relationship, interdependence and respective responsibilities of the procuring Department of Government, the Ministry of Defence, and of the sponsoring Department, usually the Department of

Trade and Industry, have never been resolved entirely satisfactorily. In World War II, Lord Beaverbrook's Ministry of Aircraft Production was responsible to Government for the manufacture by industry of the aircraft that the Royal Air Force needed. In the postwar years this system of "dual control" was maintained by means of a succession of Ministries with similar functions – Supply, Aviation, Technology and Trade and Industry – operating in parallel with the Ministry of Defence to ensure that the industrial and economic interests of the relevant aerospace companies who produced equipment for the Royal Air Force and the other Services were safeguarded.

In the cases of Supply and Aviation these two Ministries actually fulfilled the procurement function on behalf of the Ministry of Defence, placing orders, monitoring progress and being responsible to Government for the efficient, economic and punctual production of the defence equipment specified. During Edward Heath's term as Prime Minister Derek Rayner (now Lord Rayner), was seconded from Marks and Spencer to review the defence equipment procurement process and the Procurement Executive of the Ministry of Defence was established at his recommendation. It endures to this day. Yet although the Ministry of Defence supposedly now has "in house" control over the procurement of equipment and armaments, the process is occasionally far from smooth, especially when it comes into conflict with the policy and attitudes of the other Ministry involved in funding through launch aid the civil sector of the aerospace industry, namely the Department of Trade and Industry.

The Westland crisis was the classic case of such an intergovernmental clash. The Department of Trade and Industry's position was in line with that agreed by the Cabinet as a whole, that the Westland Company should be left alone to sort out its own financial problems. It could be argued that those financial problems were manifestly forseeable well in advance and therefore that the company would be able to put a strategy in place to remedy them, which is what occurred by means of an equity capital injection from the Italian Fiat and American Sikorski companies.

The Ministry of Defence gave great weight to the merits of securing Britain's participation in new European collaborative helicopter programmes in addition to the EH 101, namely the possible five-nation NH 90 transport helicopter and the possible four-nation Agusta 129 Mk2 light attack helicopter, by proposing the acceptance of unquantified financial support from a so-called "European Consortium" of European helicopter manufacturers (all of whom suffered from existing overcapacity) plus British Aerospace.

In the event, the view of the Board of Westland and that of the British Government as a whole, that the rescue of the company by Fiat and Sikorski would not constitute any impediment to Westland's involvement in collaborative studies and projects with European partners, was vindicated. While the Ministry of Defence was right to demonstrate its concern that Westland, the sole domestic supplier of helicopters, should for strategic reasons remain in business, it was wrong to involve itself in the promotion of a particular solution to the company's commercial problems against the judgement of the Board and contrary to the decision of the Cabinet as a whole.

It is not to be expected that a crisis of a similar kind would arise again. There were extraordinary personality and political characteristics to the whole Westland Affair which were unique. Furthermore the Ministry of Defence should prove more reluctant to interfere in a supplier's internal commercial problems. Without doubt, after the critical publicity about this damaging episode and the recommendations of the Select Committee on Defence, both the Ministry of Defence and the Department of Trade and Industry should be alert to the importance of anticipating such problems and of agreeing solutions will in advance, even without the superimposition of an Aerospace Board to co-ordinate formally the policies of the two Departments.

It is noteworthy that the debate on the Select Committee Report on Westland in the House of Commons in the autumn of 1986 was characterised by a highly charged political atmosphere about leaks, the rôle of the Solicitor General and No. 10 Downing Street. The debate on the European helicopter industry in WEU was by contrast far more technically detailed, better informed and serious. The work of the House of Commons Select Committee on Defence on Westland was superb. The performance of the House in the Chamber veered from hysteria to hyperbole and back again, which emphasises the importance of Select Committee work for serious consideration of specialist issues.

The problems of the European helicopter industry as a whole are by no means resolved. Its overcapacity could even become worse owing to the determination of the Spanish and Dutch to become involved in helicopter manufacture. However, both the Westland affair in England and a less publicised, but nevertheless significant, failure of France and West Germany to establish a viable collaborative anti-tank helicopter programme, have demonstrated the need for European collaboration in this important field of high technology and of concerting operational requirements for helicopters in Europe.

It is true that the Europeans have been slow to realise the tactical importance of the helicopter in the land/air battle; it is also true that the industry is far weaker than its counterpart in the United States, not just for lack of military orders but owing to an infinitely smaller civilian market. Nevertheless, the failure until recently of the Europeans to concert a military helicopter strategy has cost them dear. Now both the NH 90 and the Agusta 129 Mk2 could become realities. The EH 101 has potential as a transport aircraft for the Royal Air Force and not just as an anti-submarine helicopter for the Royal Navy. The Black Hawk, if built under licence by Westland, and powered with the Rolls-Royce – Turbomeca RTM 322 engine, could have a market with overseas customers as a light support helicopter replacement.

Even so the whole process of readjustment of the helicopter industry has been unnecessarily traumatic in Europe, and in Britain dramatically so. Foresight and a determination to harmonise operational requirements and re-equipment timescales among the European members of NATO could have obviated most of the problems which were exacerbated in the United Kingdom by extraordinary lethargy on the part of the Defence Staff. Such lethargy demonstrated itself also over the remarkable controversy about Airborne Early Warning for the Royal Air Force.

The Nimrod AEW Fiasco

The Nimrod AEW cancellation followed a substantial cost overrun, serious delay in entry into Royal Air Force service, and major failure to meet the Royal Air Force's specification for an Airborne Early Warning Aircraft set out in Air Staff Requirement 400. A British decision in favour of the Boeing E3A Airborne Early Warning and Control System (AWACS) ought, with hindsight, to have been made in 1978 when the NATO AWACS force was ordered. How such a small production run of eleven Nimrod Mk.3 AEW could ever have been cost effective is hard to understand. Furthermore, it seems extraordinary that the United Kingdom deliberately chose at the outset to deny itself the benefits of interoperability, standardisation, common training, logistic and infrastructural support which participation in the NATO AWACS force would have offered.

The irony is that the Ministry of Defence allowed itself to be persuaded in 1977 that the indecision over the NATO AWACS force was so intractable that the immediate initiation of the Nimrod AEW Mk.3 programme was essential if the Royal Air Force's urgent requirement for a modern Airborne Early Warning system was to be met in time. In the event, the NATO AWACS programme was launched in 1978, a year later than the Nimrod Mk.3, and yet AWACS has been operational from Geilenkirchen in the Federal Republic of Germany since 1982, whilst the three Nimrod Mk.3 aircraft delivered to the Royal Air Force by December 1986 – the time of cancellation – still fell far short in 1986 of reaching the operational standard and status which were expected by the Royal Air Force to be attained by 1984.

Immediate lessons are clear. Dramatic progress with the system was made by the General Electric Company (GEC) from the Spring of 1986 when the requirement was opened up to competition, when GEC was made prime contractor, and when the previous cost plus contract was terminated. Cost plus contracts should only be approved by the Ministry of Defence in the most exceptional circumstances, collaborative solutions or joint purchase of most major weapon systems should be the normal procurement process for reasons of security of delivery as well as shared development and support costs. Competitive tendering, the official Ministry of Defence policy, has been shown to be indispensable. One of Heseltine's most important reforms, it should have been instituted long ago. It has fully proved its worth.

Finally, the dangers of the obsessive secrecy of the Ministry of Defence have been made patently plain by the Nimrod fiasco. Some Members of Parliament did know of the problem of Nimrod Mk.3 AEW literally years before its cancellation but could not divulge all they knew because they would have breached confidences of serving Royal Air Force officers who were potentially in breach of the Official Secrets Act. As explained elsewhere, the establishment of a Defence Equipment Appropriations Sub-Committee of the Select Committee on Defence of the House of Commons is indeed essential to monitor, if necessary confidentially, the progress of the most important procurements of defence equipment by the Armed Forces. Had it existed, the House of Commons would have been alerted to the problems of Nimrod Mk.3 well in advance, the taxpayer saved millions of pounds, and the interests of the Royal Air Force more effectively secured.

Collaborative Successes

By contrast, most collaborative programmes have proved successful. The Tornado GR1 aircraft has proved one of the outstanding collaborative successes of its generation. This aircraft has won bombing competitions for the Royal Air Force in the United States against the premier crews of the United States Air Force. The controversies over Westland and Nimrod Mk.3 merit examination, but they are not typical of the defence procurement business, although important lessons can be derived from both. Above all, the Ministry of Defence, by revealing more about costs and timescales to elected Members of Parliament and by making tendering a more open process, could naturally avoid crises very largely of their own making as over Nimrod Mk.3. The relationship between Parliament and Government need not be adversarial. There are merits in Government's taking selected Members of Parliament into its confidence on these matters.

Future projects such as the European Fighter Aircraft, new helicopters, possible new Assault Ships and potentially even a European Anti Tactical Ballistic Missile system, these are the kinds of major programmes which could merit scrutiny by a Defence Appropriations Sub Committee of the House of Commons. They are high risk technology projects, although in the case of ATBMs and Assault Ships not yet initiated, and all would have major economic and employment implications. An important area for the future is military space technology which recently hit the headlines in an unexpected way.

Project ZIRCON

In January 1987 the "New Statesman" Magazine revealed that the United Kingdom had been developing a secret military intelligence gathering satellite system, codenamed Project ZIRCON, and made much of the fact that Parliament was unaware of this project just as it had at first received no intimation of the development of The Chevaline Multiple Warhead System for the Polaris missiles in the late 1970s. Here was another possible example of the need for the establishment of a machinery of routine accountability by Government to Parliament for the development of projects of this kind, although it must be said that the project had the highest security classification and that details of its technology and performance would have had to remain secret.

A parliamentary row could have been avoided if from the inception of the intelligence gathering satellite project a Defence Appropriations Sub Committee of the Defence Select Committee had been able to monitor its progress and satisfy itself about the expenditure of public money involved. At present the Comptroller and Auditor General has to notify the Public Accounts Committee of the House of Commons only when the expenditure on a single defence project exceeds £250 million.

However, the announcement to the public of a project of considerable military merit and great industrial significance was marred by familiarly obsessive Governmental secrecy and once secrecy was blown, by one of Britain's traditional "whodunnit" witch hunts. Public attention focussed on news reports of raids by Special Branch on the "New Statesman's" journalist's flat and on the BBC in Glasgow, on the Speaker of the House of Commons' action in banning the showing of a film on the project to MPs within the Palace of Westminster, consequent debates, and the arcane rôle of the Attorney General in securing the necessary legal injunction to "safeguard the public interest."

As far back as 1980 the Assembly of Western European Union passed a Report by one of the authors of this book calling for a European Surveillance Satellite System.[8] Subsequent WEU reports by the author concerned and above all the seminar in Munich in September, 1985 sponsored by the Committee on Scientific, Technological and Aerospace Questions of the Assembly of Western European Union on "*The Space Challenge for Europe*", emphasised the need for Europe to exploit space technology for military purposes and to develop its own space based military equipments and systems.

The United Kingdom has considerable expertise already in satellite telecommunications through its Skynet series of military communications satellites, an expertise that has been recognised by NATO in the award to British Aerospace of a contract for a new telecommunications satellite system, NATO IV. France too has militarily relevant experience, gained from the construction of its national civil remote sensing satellite system, SPOT, as have many member nations of the European Space Agency, including Britain, who have been collaborating on the development of the first European civil remote sensing satellite system ERS 1.

It was hardly surprising therefore that the United Kingdom should be involved in the development of a new military satellite for gathering signals intelligence (ZIRCON), particularly so since the British operational reputation for excellence in this field is high, first from operations at Bletchley Park in World War Two and latterly, from the work of the Government Communications Headquarters (GCHQ) at Cheltenham. That ZIRCON should be a purely national project is, in some ways, surprising since there would be cost savings in a collaborative development. However, the United Kingdom has never shown publicly, at least, any serious interest in a European military space programme. Unlike the United States, where space technologies have made an important strategic impact, military planning in Britain is not much affected by military developments in space.

The Assembly of Western European Union has argued the merits of a European military space programme for many years, as well as the merits of a joint European response to the Strategic Defence Initiative (SDI). These pleas and well researched arguments have fallen largely on deaf ears.

The problem has been partly institutional since the greater part of the United Kingdom's space effort is channelled through the European Space Agency (ESA) which by its statute of foundation is precluded from engaging in military space programmes. The other institutional difficulty is that the United Kingdom has been lukewarm towards the Western European Union ever since its reactivation at Rome in October, 1984, in spite of the fact that four of the WEU member nations, Britain, France, West Germany and Italy are the principal countries with highly developed space industries in Europe and in spite of the fact that WEU's specialist agencies, as well as its Parliamentary Assembly, lend to it substantial practical advantages in addition to its competence by treaty to concert a strategy for Europe on military space applications.

Liaison between the Assembly of Western European Union and the European Space Agency is already exceptionally close. Both are located in Paris and the Assembly of WEU has always comprehended the strategic importance of the work sponsored by the ESA. Most of Europe's principal space programmes have been collaborative, such as the Ariane Launcher, Spacelab, Meteosat and so on. The main European effort in space in the future will be collaborative – the Columbus module to the NASA space station, the Ariane V launcher, the Hermes reusable space vehicle, perhaps HOTOL also. It is important that the military relevance of Europe's space programme is not overlooked. Those members of ESA's Ministerial council belonging to WEU nations could join their Defence Minister counterparts on the WEU Ministerial council on a regular basis to orchestrate a military space programme for Europe, and ensure that there is strategic relevance to Europe's space activities.

The United Kingdom has already taken an imaginative initiative in the establishment in 1986 of the British National Space Centre at Farnborough specifically to co-ordinate the civil and military elements of the United Kingdom space programme. On a national scale such co-ordination will ensure that the maximum benefit is obtained from the meagre resources allocated by Britain in the space field. Britain should take the lead in seeking to overcome the inhibitions of its European allies in NATO about the necessity for a European military space programme.

Satellite communications, reconnaissance, intelligence gathering, anti satellite systems, ballistic missile technology, launchers and manned recoverable space vehicles all these and many other areas of space activity could be of military benefit to Europe. The British HOTOL project could be assigned a number of military missions and it is to be hoped that planning for this is already going ahead.

If it is serious about its defence, Europe and not just the United States, will need to ensure that Soviet satellites are not inviolate. European nations should study as a matter of urgency whether they may wish to procure the anti satellite missile system launched by the American F.15 fighter and whether it can be adapted to the Tornado F3 or whether they will need to develop a comparable system of their own. The "eyes and ears" which satellite systems constitute to potentially hostile nations will have to be denied to them in time of war, and Europe will require the means to do so.

Strategic Defence Against Ballistic Missiles

Strategic defence is of great importance for Europe's security and not merely an obsessive and unrealistic preoccupation of our American allies of little significance to the defence of Europe. Anti-ballistic missile defence will become increasingly feasible technically and just because it can never be totally effective, this is no justification for not developing, building and putting in place such defence. There is nothing dramatically novel about protecting the nuclear deterrent in Western Europe against pre-emptive attacks.

In the 1950s and 1960s, when the B47 and B52 bombers of Strategic Air Command provided the ultimate nuclear guarantee of Europe's defence, and during the time when the V Bomber force of Royal Air Force Bomber Command and the Mirage IV aircraft of the *Armée de l'Air* constituted the British and French strategic nuclear deterrent forces, there was no criticism of the deployment of fighter aircraft to protect the bomber bases.

When, towards the end of the 1960s, the expanding Soviet space programme was beginning to yield results in the growth of the Soviet Union's offensive rocket forces, the building of a chain of early warning stations against possible Soviet ballistic missile attack was regarded as a normal, prudent measure, and the inauguration of the BMEW facility at Fylingdales in Yorkshire was uncontroversial.

The more fearsome the weapons of mass destruction, the more important is it to reduce the vulnerability of defence installations and civilian populations alike. The deployment of sensors in space to detect the launch of ballistic missiles, can only be regarded as a confidence building initiative which would lessen the risk of surprise attack. This could be the kind of military space programme of significance to Europe's defence, whether as part of an Alliance-wide post SDI deployment or as a unilateral European project.

The development of point defence anti-ballistic missile systems was almost totally ended by the Anti-Ballistic Missile Treaty of 1972 in the West, although not in the Soviet Union. The treaty was concluded between the Superpowers because the increased accuracy of ballistic missiles and the development of multiple independently targetable re-entry vehicles (MIRVs) gave to the offense an ability to strike surely and with precision, whereas the defence was inordinately expensive and uncertain.

Now the maintenance of the Anti-Ballistic Missile Treaty of 1972 is rather more an issue of relevance to the overall strategic balance between the Superpowers and the delicate diplomatic process of arms control, than primarily a matter of economic and technical convenience. Its invocation is part of the routine anti SDI rhetoric of Soviet arms control negotiators.

The Short Range Missile Threat to Europe

Whereas space based defences against ballistic missiles remain extremely futuristic in spite of the SDI research programme and whereas new interception techniques, such as directed energy weapons, are very far from being satisfactorily proven in tests, let alone near to operational deployment, one aspect of an overall strategic defence architecture appears more feasible, namely, point defence against incoming ballistic missiles in the terminal phase.

Not only does this fact open up possibilities of worthwhile research and technical co-operation by British companies under the aegis of the United States SDI programme. More importantly, work on point defence systems in the context of a European Defence Initiative (EDI) on the part of European aerospace companies is highly germane to the urgent need to counter the growing threat to much of Western Europe posed by the deployment by the Soviet Union of short range ballistic missile systems – SS21s, SS22s and SS23s in the German Democratic Republic and Czechoslovakia.

This force of new offensive weapons, which are accurate enough to be effective with conventional warheads as well as nuclear, has been built by the USSR since the modernisation of NATO's intermediate range nuclear forces under the "twin-track decision" of 1979 whereby ground launched Cruise Missiles and Pershing II ballistic missiles were deployed by NATO from December, 1983. If, following the Reyjkavik summit, the Zero Option were to be invoked by the United States and Soviet Union and SS20s in the Western military districts of the Soviet Union withdrawn and both Pershing II rockets and GLCMs withdrawn by NATO from Belgium, Britain, the Federal Republic of Germany, Holland and Italy, then the vulnerability of the heart of Western Europe to Soviet SS21s, SS22s and SS23s would be enhanced, as was implicity acknowledged in the communiqué issued at the conclusion of the meeting at Camp David, Maryland, between Prime Minister Thatcher and President Reagan in November, 1986.

This imbalance in short range systems, which is serious enough already, will have to be redressed offensively by the deployment on the part of NATO of countervailing, if not exactly equivalent, forces such as stand off air to surface guided weapons for Tornado strike/attack aircraft of the Italian, West German and Royal Air Forces. It will also have to be redressed defensively, first by traditional passive measures of improved dispersal, hardening and concealment of NATO's key air assets as well as by improved redundancy of NATO's command and control facilities. Secondly, the imbalance caused by the new Soviet short range ballistic missile systems will have to be actively countered by the development, manufacture and deployment of point defence systems on the part of the European members of NATO, to protect their key installations against surprise pre-emptive short range ballistic missile attack on the part of the Warsaw Pact.

Vulnerability never did enhance deterrence, a strategic reality which the Soviets have always clearly comprehended as their deployment of a modernised anti-ballistic missile system around Moscow and elaborate civil defence measures plainly demonstrate. The Soviet leadership has never accepted that the doctrine of Mutual Assured Destruction should apply to them or to the Soviet people. Soviet war planning and exercises are predicated on the possibility of the uşe of nuclear weapons at the outset of any conflict and on the premise that such a conflict should be survivable for the Soviet people.

Vulnerability reduces the credibility of deterrence, and exposes Western Europe to nuclear intimidation and blackmail. The SDI further reinforces the overall level of deterrence available to the Western Alliance. Ballistic missile defences eliminate the assurance for a potential agrressor that a particular warhead can eliminate a particular target. Retaliation is therefore made more certain and the risk of pre-emptive attack reduced.

If a reasonably reliable defence against ballistic missiles could be deployed in the United States, Europe's American allies would be more likely, not, as so often argued, less likely, to invoke the United States' nuclear guarantee on behalf of Western Europe in the knowledge that to do so would not necessarily entail the obliteration of the homeland of the

United States. The coupling between the European and American pillars of the North Atlantic Alliance would be strengthened, and both components of the North Atlantic Community of free nations rendered more secure against a surprise Soviet attack.

CHAPTER VII

A New Strategy for the Western Alliance

In the lifetime of NATO the global strategic scene has changed fundamentally; the process of change is continuing and its speed increasing. A contribution to the defence of the NATO area is no longer the totally dominant overseas commitment of the USA nor is that area any more the most sensitive sector of its forward defence. The course of world events has obliged the West's superpower to scan not only its eastern horizon but those to the west and south as well in its watch for threats to national security. This extended surveillance is also necessary to pursue the political and strategic objectives of what has become a global commitment for the Western Alliance, namely the containment of Soviet imperialism and international communism.

The increasing military burdens of the Alliance's predominant member, which this commitment creates, require changes in the relationship of Washington with its European allies and in the manner in which they share the military tasks of the defence of the NATO area. This situation presents Western Europe with a challenge for which it has so far shown little enthusiasm, but the political pressure within the United States for such changes can be expected to grow and should not be ignored by West European Governments. In the words of the leading potential Democratic Presidential Candidate in the United States, Gary Hart,

> *"It's nonsense to keep talking about preserving NATO as it is. NATO's not good enough and it can't be fixed without the Allies spending a great deal more money and without us spending our money differently."*[1]

During the past twenty years the economic growth of the Pacific Basin countries, headed by the spectacular performance of Japan, has far outstripped that of Western Europe. North American exports to these countries now equal those to Europe and the Pacific Ocean now carries more trade than the Atlantic. The dominance of the Japanese currency in the world's financial markets had already been discussed (see page 23). The policy of Premier Nakasone is to achieve a political rôle for his country which is in keeping with its economic strength and acceptable to domestic public opinion and to neighbouring States.

Understandably, Washington would like to see a greater Japanese defence effort forming part of this more self-confident role. The economic growth of the Pacific basin has been matched by an increase in its strategic importance and the expansion of the Soviet Pacific Fleet shows that Moscow is aware of this development. With the increased range of Russian intercontinental nuclear missiles, the potential usefulness of the Pacific as a launching area for submarine-based strategic weapons has added to United States strategic concern for the region.

Inevitably, as the machinery of the Gramm-Rudman-Hollings legislation for reduction of the federal deficit begins to slice at the Reagan administration's defence procurement programmes – a process now unlikely to be impeded by Congress – the Pentagon will be faced with the unwelcome need to establish strategic priorities in the global task of containment and threat coverage.

TABLE 7.1
UNITED STATES ARMED FORCES GLOBAL DEPLOYMENT 1986–87
(Uniformed Personnel, 000s)

Service	Strength	USA (Incl: Central America, Caribbean & Atlantic Ocean)	Europe (West Germany)	Middle East & Indian Ocean	Pacific & Far East
ARMY	**770.9**	**501.6**	**217.1** **(209.0)**	**1.2**	**51.0**
NAVY	**570.9**	**406.3**	**55.1** **(–)**	**14.8**	**94.7**
MARINE CORPS	**196.3**	**152.1**	**3.2** **(–)**	–	**41.0**
AIR FORCE	**605.8**	**379.2**	**92.7** **(41.1)**	–	**133.9**
TOTALS	**2,143.9**	**1,439.2**	**368.1** **(250.1)**	**16.0**	**320.6**
PERCENT AGE	**100.0**	**67.1**	**17.2**	**0.7**	**15.0**

(**Source:** "*The Military Balance 1986–87*". International Institute for Strategic Studies. London)

This need for strategic priorities will be strengthened by growing criticisms that the Reagan Administration's defence policy has lacked those very priorities, that in attempting to implement a strategy of global military containment of Soviet expansion it has failed to examine sufficiently the nature of the long-term Soviet threat and the likely intentions of Moscow in implementing it; has possibly even exaggerated this threat; and has paid too little attention to the already discernable problems which will follow from the inevitable cuts in United States defence spending over the next decade. As one United States commentator succinctly pointed out when discussing the idea of a new regular-reserve forces mix for NATO as part of an alliance burden-sharing plan:

> *"The issue, however, is how much is militarily sufficient at politically sustainable levels of support."*[2]

Stagnation in Europe

Continuing economic growth in the Pacific Basin will be matched by relative stagnation in Western Europe. Despite the fall in energy and raw material costs national economies seem unable to break out strongly from the plateau of productivity and comfortable living standards reached at the end of the seventies. Unemployment remains high, and social security costs continue to rise in consequence. The financially greedy monster which the EEC's Common Agricultural Policy has become threatens to bankrupt the Community if not reined in.

> *"The CAP is an absolutely intolerable policy, and at the same time an absolutely indispensable one . . . It is Europe's sacred cow, an uncontrollable cornucopia which threatens to overwhelm those who conjured it up with an unmanageable largesse of corn and beef, butter, olives and wine."*[3]

In 1986 the CAP budget of about £12 billion representing the costs of production subsidies and of storing the ever rising stocks of surplus food was expected to over-run by at least £1 billion. Taking the rate of $1.4 to £1 which ruled at the end of November 1986, the cost of this budget was some ten per cent more than the 1986 defence budgets both of France and of the Federal Republic of Germany expressed in dollar terms.

In these conditions, it is hardly surprising that, as in the USA, the era of annual real increases in NATO European defence budgets has ended. Indeed in some countries despite lower rates of domestic inflation there is now negative real growth in defence spending. Here lies the cause of the low nuclear threshold in Europe, of the philosophy of the "short war", and of increased acceptance of the inevitability of early escalation to a nuclear response in the event of Warsaw Pact attack.

From these economic roots, too, spring the fears for the future security of the NATO area expressed after the 1986 super power Summit at Reykjavik had floated ideas for the abolition of all strategic ballistic missiles within ten years and for the total elimination of intermediate-range nuclear forces (INF) from both sides of the Iron Curtain.

Thus it was that in 1987 the future of the British independent strategic nuclear deterrent force became not only the subject of acrimonious domestic political debate, but more significantly a factor of growing importance in the complex issues of European defence and strategic policy.

Deterrence and the Nuclear Threshold. A Strategic Variable

Over the years, the debate on nuclear arms has come to dominate the arena of strategic argument, but this emphasis on what is but a part of the wider field of deterrence in all its forms distorts such argument and neglects the equally important question of conventional arms and their value in the continuous struggle to preserve the peace whilst at the same time safeguarding the strategic objectives of the Western Alliance. Any examination of the global strategic scene in the 1980s has to assume that nuclear weapons are here to stay until the unattainable millennium is reached when a totally successful outcome of the SDI research project renders them obsolete.

Deterrence must therefore continue to comprise both conventional and nuclear elements, and the doctrine of flexible response remains as satisfactory a way as can be devised of preparing a realistic defence policy for an alliance possessing a nuclear capability. It follows that the nuclear threshold will continue to be a factor in the strategic equation, with its level determined not only by the conventional military capabilities of the Western Alliance in relation to those of the Soviet Union and her satellites and surrogates but also by an appraisal of the Soviet view of the strategic importance to its potential adversaries of particular areas or theatres and therefore of its judgment on the likelihood of a nuclear response to any conventional act of aggression.

In the context of a policy of overall containment of Soviet global aspirations it has now become necessary for the Western Alliance to examine the minimum levels of nuclear threshold required in those areas where Soviet/Warsaw Pact conventional forces – in place or rapidly deployable – pose a military threat to its territories or vital interests.

Nowhere is this strategic reassessment more needed than in considering the overall defence of the NATO area against the multi-dimensional threat now posed by the deployment of modern, highly capable Soviet and Warsaw Pact conventional forces (land, sea, and air) not only in the central region but adjacent to other sectors of the NATO front as well, especially in the northern area. The adoption of this broader strategic perspective by NATO has become essential in preparing its future plans for, as the London *Times* pithily foresaw:

> *"The ossification of so much military argument about Central European force levels now needs some decisive corrective."*[4]

NATO should now accept the *fait accompli* brought about by the refusal of its members to match the Warsaw Pact threat on the Central Front on a gun for gun and a tank for tank basis and by the resulting priority now given to the maintenance of the nuclear element of deterrence of an attack on this sector. In the existing nuclear situation of the superpowers, this refusal may come to be regarded as a strategically realistic and economical policy. It has turned the central region into an area where the present relatively low nuclear threshold (as measured by the Warsaw Pact/NATO conventional imbalance) is acceptable since Soviet perceptions of the strategic importance of the area to the Alliance and of the consequent probability of an early nuclear response to a conventional attack makes such an initiative unlikely. After all, this is the case on which the political claim that nuclear deterrent forces have kept the peace in Europe for forty years is founded.

Elsewhere there should be a similar review of the factors which determine what level of conventional force is needed (and what type of force) to maintain a viable nuclear threshold over the whole NATO area. In this review account must be taken of the fact that in considering new military measures to tilt the present geo-strategic balance within the NATO area in their favour Soviet planners now have the benefit of conventional forces greatly improved in their reach and in their weapon power to draw on. Such measures could test the credibility of the European nuclear deterrent forces with less risk than would be incurred by action on the central front. In this scenario there are threats not only to NATO's flanks (particularly to Scandinavia in the north and to the Balkans in the south), but also to other vital interests of the Western Alliance outside the NATO area.

In the context of European defence this concept of a changeable prescription of conventional and nuclear deterrence varied to suit the differing strategic circumstances within the NATO area is developed further below (see pages 103). It is the basis of the proposed triphibious strategic plan for the conventional defence of the NATO area, its territory, ocean and sea approaches, and air space.

Looking Ahead

In the absence of unforseen political developments the Western Alliance will remain under the domination of the USA for the rest of this century at least. But for economic reasons even the West's superpower will be obliged to establish strategic priorities in the allocation of its gradually declining conventional defence resources. In determining these priorities an assessment on a global basis of long-erm Soviet strategic aims will be necessary as will an examination of how the considerable military assets of the Allies can be deployed in the most cost-effective manner to assist the USA in its containment policy.

The United States should seek the participation of its allies in these strategic assessments and in discussions on sharing the military burdens of the Alliance. They represent the substance of the case for a Western strategic summit conference, the composition of which should mirror that of the now customary annual economic summits of the Western industrialised nations and Japan, for in the end it is the state of the economic health of its members as much as the military threats with which it is faced that determines the ability of the Alliance to support its strategy with sufficient armed strength. The idea of a strategic summit has already been mooted by the authors.[5] The subsequent course of world events has rendered its convening even more important especially with the growing imminence of elections on both sides of the Atlantic the results of which may – and in the case of the USA will cause changes in the cast of political leaders in whose hands the future of the Western Alliance rests.

The Future of NATO

A strategic summit called to examine Western strategy on a global basis would provide a forum for the United States to expound its views on military-burden-sharing and to explain the likely future division of its conventional defence resources between the European-Atlantic and Pacific regions. More detailed work would then be needed to determine the complex problems of the future of NATO. The views of Senator Hart quoted at the head of this chapter reflect the growing study of this subject now being undertaken in the USA.

Washington perceives, perhaps more clearly than its European allies, the need for a new strategic relationship with those allies, based on the economic and strategic circumstances of the 1980s rather than on those of the 1950s as at present. In the United States view the basis of such a relationship would be the exploitation of the latent European ability to improve its defence effort by sensible but not necessarily expensive reforms, particularly improved interoperability of forces through weapon and equipment standardisation, and more collaboration in military production and research and development. The shadow of the 1982 Roth-Glenn-Nunn Amendment still hangs over NATO Europe; after 1988 it may prove to be more substance and less shadow.[6]

The challenge to Western Europe will result from a United States decision – by 1987 considered in many quarters to be increasingly likely after the next Presidential election – to reduce its military presence in Europe, even if only by a token amount. A request from Washington for an improved European defence effort could accompany the announcement of this decision. How Europe deals with these developments will determine the adequacy of its response to the American challenge.

Were events to unfold in this way, a role for the United Kingdom as honest broker and middleman can be discerned. Britain, France and West Germany form the natural body of NATO Europe, the limbs of which are the flank allies to north and south and in the Iberian Peninsula. This trio forms the most powerful grouping in Western Europe, a grouping round which the foundations of a new indigenous European defence policy could be laid. A pre-emptive discussion by President Mitterand, Chancellor Kohl and Prime Minister Thatcher and their advisers on the issues of defence and deterrence in Europe as the twenty-first century dawns could appease any bouts of United States isolationism and frustration with the European Allies ahead of the Presidential election and before any Western strategic summit might take place. A United Kingdom initiative to convene such a meeting would enable London to put forward its ideas on a new strategy for the defence of the NATO area and on a new and financially affordable British role in such a strategy. Another turning point in the post-war history of European defence collaboration would have been reached.

Towards a European Defence Policy

A political initiative on these lines would inevitably raise amongst the countries of Western Europe the broader question of what is about to become the foremost geo-strategic issue facing the Western Alliance, namely the future defence and strategic relationship between the USA and the European allies.

Can an indigenous West European defence policy be agreed amongst the NATO European countries (and equally important be subsequently maintained without serious internal rupture) so as to give them a stronger position and a more influential role in the conduct of NATO, to transform its organisation, so that it displays less elements of superpower domination and more those of a partnership between two equals united in a common strategic purpose and still pledged to come to each other's assistance in the event of an act of aggression?

At the heart of the problems raised by this immensely complex question lies the extraordinary dichotomy of a group of advanced industrialised nations, amongst them some of the most prosperous in the world, united economically by the Treaty of Rome but lacking that essential component of a normal alliance, a common defence and strategic policy. NATO was not designed to provide the framework for such a policy but merely to institutionalise the commitment of the United States to the defence of what was, at the time, a war-weakened Europe against an act of aggression by Soviet Russia and her satellites.

If the collective wish of an economically stronger and politically more confident Europe is now to seek a role as a strong political force and strategic group, ranking only below the two superpowers in the table of global power precedence, then the leaders of the countries concerned will have to ponder more deeply than they have done so far on how to achieve that unanimity in foreign and defence policies which would be essential to the success of such aspirations, and what economic and political sacrifices would have to be made at national levels to the cause of collective European security and influence.

In the course of 1986, two dramatic events emphasised the complexity of the issues involved and how far Europe, in its present state of strategic disorganisation, would have to travel to reach the desired destination. The pusillanimous and divided reactions of the EEC countries to the American raids on Libya in April of that year exposed to public view the difficulties of reaching agreement on an important international issue, the combating of terrorism, amongst the members of what is still an economic rather than a political community. With such ineffectual political machinery, it was clear that the EEC was not the forum in which to draw up a co-ordinated European defence and strategic policy, a task which, in fairness, it was never designed to accomplish.

But there was a more serious aspect to the Libyan affair. At issue was a unilateral action by the United States, the ally of Western Europe, the super- power under the defence umbrella of which, wearing their NATO hats, the majority of these selfsame Community members had been happy to shelter for nigh on forty years. As the London *Times* pointed out:

> *"But the embryonic structure of EEC co-ordination exposed another division: that between Europe and the United States, with Britain uneasily in the middle. In this respect the EEC could prove to be an obstacle to the unity of the North Atlantic Treaty Organisation, to which most of the 12 belong. . . . the countries of Europe would do well to contemplate the possibility that an all-European foreign policy and the continuing authority of NATO may eventually prove incompatible."*[7]

In October, the European Allies suffered another fit of strategic malaise. The suggestion emanating from the Reykjavik summit of a possible super-power agreement to phase out all long-range nuclear ballistic missiles over ten years raised grave suspicions of United States indifference to European security where issues of superpower diplomacy were involved. The subsequent mission by the British Prime Minister, in which she was successful in obtaining Presidential reassurances on this matter, whilst helpful in the short term, once again renewed European discussion of the strategic relationship with the USA and of what the position of Europe might be if the superpower arms reduction dialogue was eventually to yield tangible results.

Despite United Kingdom leadership of the campaign for a robust and united EEC policy to fight international terrorism, by the end of 1986 there had been a little sign of any desire on the part of the British Conservative Government to initiate discussions on the closer co-ordination of European defence policies and on a new strategy for the defence of the NATO area in which the European allies might play a more predominant part. Across the Channel, however, France was displaying more interest in these matters.

During the spring of 1986, President Mitterand and Chancellor Kohl agreed a number of measures to improve Franco-German military co-operation in the interests of European defence. At the end of February, in a joint communiqué, the two countries announced their agreement on operational co-operation between their armed forces, and on studies relating to the best employment of French forces in Germany including the Force d'Action Rapide (FAR). During 1987 the largest joint military exercise undertaken by the two countries since World War II will take place with participation both by the FAR and by units from the French 2nd Army in Germany. German approval of these developments was confirmed by Hans-Dietrich Genscher, the Foreign Minister, who described them as "the nucleus of the crystallization of a European defence policy"[8]

The concept of the FAR itself also blazes an innovative trail in European military practice pointing to the type of flexible and mobile rapid deployment land/air forces which will be increasingly required in future to deal with the threats which can now develop in any part of the European front or indeed to safeguard vital NATO interests "out of area".

TABLE 7.2
FRANCE 1986
Composition of the Force Action Rapide (FAR)

HQ Maisons – Laffitte
Total strength: 47,000

Formation	Composition
4th Air Mobile Division (Nancy) Strength 5,100	2 inf, 4 combat helicopter regts, 1 comd/sp regt, 1 log bde. Total: 204 support, manoeuvre and gunship helicopters
6th Light Armoured Division (Nímes) Strength 7,400	2 lt armd, 2 APC inf, 1 arty, 1 eng, 1 comd/sp regt. Total: 72 AMX 10 armd recce vehs, 24 155mm(SP) guns and 48 surface-air missiles
11th Parachute Division (Toulouse) Strength 13,500	6 para inf regts, 1 eng. regt, 1 lt armour regt, 1 comd/spt regt, 1 arty regt, 1spt bn
9th Air Portable Marine Infantry Division (Nantes) Strength 8,000	4 motorised inf regts, 1 lt armd regt with anti-armour sqdn, 1 arty, 1 eng, 1 comd/spt regt
27th Alpine Division (Grenoble) Strength 8,500	6 mountain regts, with Milan anti-armour weapons 1 lt armd regt, 1 arty regt with 24 105mm guns, 1 eng bn, 1 comd/spt regt plus surface-air missiles

An Enlarged Role for Western European Union?

Before the year was out there were further signs of French interest in the future of West European security. Evidently persuaded of the unsuitability of the EEC as a forum for the management of a more closely co-ordinated European defence policy, Jacques Chirac, the Prime Minister, repeated with more conviction the 1984 French suggestion that Western European Union (WEU) should assume responsibility for this task. In an address to its Assembly in Paris on December 2nd, he proposed the drawing up of what might be called the "Western European Charter of Security Principles" to which he was convinced the seven members of the organisation would be able to agree.[9] The importance of these proposals as the basis on which a new European defence and strategic policy for the defence of the NATO area could be drawn up merits their reproduction in full:

> *"Nuclear deterrence remains the only effective way of preventing war in Europe. There is no alternative to it in the foreseeable future. Any developments which are likely to occur as a result of technical progress must aim to reinforce deterrence, not to bring it into question.*
> *"The threat which hangs over Western Europe must be considered as a whole: nuclear arms of all ranges, imbalance of conventional and chemical weapons. Dissuasive capabilities and disarmament efforts must be defined in relation to this overall threat.*
> *"Deterrence in Europe requires a strategic linkage between the two sides of the Atlantic. This, in turn, requires the presence of American conventional and nuclear forces on our continent.*
> *"Maintaining the defence effort of the European states on a level in keeping with the threat is a necessity. It is also the condition for strengthening the European political bond. In this respect the contribution of the independent French and British nuclear forces is an essential factor.*
> *"The aim of disarmament must be to increase security while at the same time decreasing the number of weapons by means of realistic and verifiable agreements."*[10]

A favourable British response to the idea of a revived and reinforced WEU would help the cause of European defence and strategic policy. More importantly, it would give a much needed signal to the continental allies that Britain accepted the growing need for discussions on the revision of such policy within the NATO structure. A study of the Chirac proposals for a charter of security principles shows that there is much common ground between the two European nuclear powers in their approach to the question of an indigenous European defence policy. In particular, the emphasis on the primary importance of nuclear deterrence in the prevention of war in Europe provides the British Government with further useful support for the modernisation of its own strategic nuclear deterrent force with the Trident SLBM system.

Chirac's proposals recognised that any programme for the more effective co-ordination of European defence policy must be carried out within the fabric of the Atlantic Alliance for:

> *"A strong, united Europe, respectful of the specificity of its members, is a guarantee of vitality for the Alliance and the basis for a healthy, balanced relationship between the two sides of the Atlantic."*[11]

Coupled with his emphasis on the need for a transatlantic strategic linkage, this confirmed that there is nothing in the French vision of a more unified European defence policy gradually emerging from the work of WEU that should cause suspicion or doubts in Britain with her tradition of close ties with the USA in defence matters. Britain should, therefore, support the French initiative. Otherwise she may find herself out on a limb, torn as she has so often been before between the responsibilities to Europe implicit in EEC membership and the "special relationship" with the USA, the reality of which has been re-emphasised by the purchase of the Trident strategic nuclear deterrent system (see page 40). Indeed, when the United States raises with its allies the question of a greater defence effort in Europe more commensurate with the latter's economic strength, Britain should take advantage of this relationship to temper United States demands, especially if they include proposals for a reduction in the size of its military presence in Europe, and to explain the European viewpoint and the extent of the substantial European contribution to the defence of the NATO area.

Initially, at least, a reinforced WEU would be more suited to dealing with the material aspects of a co-ordinated European defence policy, such as weapon and equipment programmes, standardisation, and the impact of technology rather than with the more politically sensitive areas of force deployments, command arrangements, and operational plans. The emerging Paris-Bonn military accord covered these matters on a bilateral basis. Here too Britain should seek to join in on the lines already suggested (see page 98).

A tripartite agreement between London, Paris and Bonn on the principles of a new strategic plan for the defence of the NATO area (after all they are the three most powerful military powers of NATO Europe) would both prove to Washington that a European will to tackle the problem existed (sweet music in the ears of Gary Hart and Senator Sam Nunn), and enable Britain at least to reduce the burden of her Rhine Army, and the imbalance it causes to the structure of her armed forces, and to her ability to create a more cost-effective and better constituted contribution to the defence of the NATO area appropriate to the future and aligned with the principles set out by M. Chirac.

Credibility. The Vital Ingredient of Deterrence.

Acceptance of the principle that the threat to Western Europe must be considered as a whole (the second point in the Chirac charter) is essential to the preparation of any new and realistic strategic plan for the defence of the NATO area. As to the established doctrines: flexible response remains valid whilst the capacity for nuclear retaliation exists but forward defence requires a new definition for the military threat to the NATO area is now more diversified and geographically more extended than it was when NATO was founded, and its forward defences have to be correspondingly enlarged (see page 95).

The level of the nuclear threshold in Europe is no longer solely determined by the Warsaw Pact: NATO ratios of tanks, artillery and tactical aircraft in place along the central front in Germany (the numbers game). It now depends on the overall ability of NATO forces to provide a forward and in-depth defence of its territory, air space, ocean approaches and coastal waters against the multi-dimensional threat posed by the greatly enhanced capabilities of the Soviet and Warsaw Pact forces deployed throughout the European theatre. The defence of the central front is but a part – albeit still the most politically important part of the defence of the NATO area as a whole.

If there are weak spots in such a defence then the level of the nuclear threshold in those areas falls accordingly, and the Soviets, in consequence, are offered a temptation to test the credibility of the threat of nuclear retaliation by the Western Alliance. For the principle that nuclear deterrence is the only effective way of neutralising "*the threat which hangs over Western Europe*" depends crucially on the credibility of such deterrence.

> "*Credibility is, of course, the heart of flexibility in response, and credibility's essential ingredients are military capability and political will; without either it would collapse.*"[12]

The near total reliance on the effectiveness of nuclear deterrence in maintaining peace in Europe which NATO has come to accept must, by definition, change the nature, if not the principle, of the doctrine of flexible response. Greater reliance means potentially earlier use of nuclear retaliation for an act of aggression which in turn creates less flexibility in deciding how to respond to such an act. The credibility of the nuclear deterrent forces of the Western Alliance deployed in Europe, or available to NATO in defence of the NATO area, has therefore become a factor of paramount importance in its strategic posture.

Whilst the military capability for nuclear deterrence remains intact in Britain, France, and, of course, the United States, the political will to use such deterrence has to be stronger and more decisive the greater the reliance placed on it compared with that provided by conventional forces. In the case of an attack on West German territory across the Central Front, the political will to initiate a nuclear response would be stronger than it might be if Soviet Russia began an outflanking move designed to alter the strategic balance in Europe in its favour, in North Norway for example.

This assumption that the credibility of the nuclear deterrent in Europe is strongest at the centre of the whole European front and weakens towards the flanks establishes the case for maintaining the nuclear threshold at what is judged to be at least the minimum effective level throughout the NATO area and not just in the central sector of the front. Every member of the Alliance in Europe should contribute conventional land, sea and air forces and trained reserves sufficient to maintain this level of threshold. The nature and the size of these contributions should be determined by each country's needs for national security, its military traditions and expertise, its geographical location and above all the strength of its economy. The essence of burden-sharing is to organise these national contributions into a cohesive whole to provide a viable conventional shield throughout the NATO area.

There are two fundamental reasons why this diversified defence to provide an even level of nuclear threshold throughout the NATO area is now essential. The first is to lessen the chances of Soviet adventurism on the flanks or elsewhere. A combination of a weak conventional shield and a Soviet assessment of a hesitant political response to an aggressive act could cause a fatal miscalculation. Deterrence would have failed.

Secondly, although the possibility of an assault on the Central Front may now be deemed less likely than in the past, nevertheless the enormous improvements in Soviet military capabilities which have occurred during the past two decades now make it necessary to base NATO war plans on one fundamental assumption. Were such an assault on German territory ever to be launched, it would be accompanied by simultaneous attacks by aircraft, missiles and even by special assault forces on vital military installations, ports and airfields throughout NATO Europe, including the United Kingdom and the Iberian peninsula, together with mine warfare and offensives against naval forces, shipping and air transport.

This realistic threat scenario for the future is completely different from that on which NATO plans have been based for so long. These attacks could quickly cause unacceptable levels of damage to any of the NATO European countries. In these circumstances, the progress of the land battle on the Central Front would be only one of many other crisis situations where nuclear response might have to be considered.

The Western Alliance in its Global Setting

For the foreseeable future, the principal objective of the Western Alliance will be the containment, on a global basis, of the long term campaign of Soviet Russia to advance the cause of international communism and to alter in its favour the existing precarious geo-strategic balance between east and west.

A hemispherical approach helps to explain how this objective can be sustained. Dividing the world is the United States of America, the West's superpower, with strategic interests in both the two great oceans of the world, the Atlantic and the Pacific.

By this definition, in the eastern hemisphere lies the NATO area: the principles of a forward-looking plan for its defence have already been discussed. At issue here is the potential United States demand for a greater defence effort by the European Allies and the extent to which those allies will satisfy such demands by measures to create a strategic grouping of West European states and to co-ordinate more closely their national defence policies in the common cause. National economic considerations will largely determine the extent of these measures and the timescale of their introduction. Inevitably, increases in current levels of European defence spending will be necessary to finance a new strategy for the defence of the NATO area in which the European members of the Western Alliance play a greater part.

In pondering its future strategic role, Europe faces another problem. Beyond the NATO area, but mainly within its own strategic hemisphere, lie the Middle East and the continent of Africa, two areas in which Soviet Russia will continue its activities of strategic involvement and potential expansionism, the curtailment of which is at the heart of western objectives. An analysis of these activities over the years reveals a policy of political exploitation, backed where necessary by military force, to gain control of the sources of energy and raw materials on which the economies of the West continue to rely. Hitherto the United States has assumed, almost single-handed, the immense burden of committing the deploying conventional forces to counter these strategic threats to the interests of the Western Alliance beyond the artificial confines of the NATO area. The basing agreements with a number of Middle-East countries, the establishment of the Rapid Deployment Force, and the build-up and forward deployments of the US Navy bear witness to this fact.

Now the situation is changing. Defence cutbacks and the setting of new strategic priorities will become the order of the day. The effort of a near global deployment of conventional forces may prove to be unsustainable. However, for Europe the corollary to reliance on nuclear deterrence to preserve the peace in the NATO area is acceptance of the increased likelihood of Soviet adventurism beyond Europe where a low or non-existent nuclear threshold is perceived yet where interests at least as vital to Europe as to the USA can be threatened. Surely a militarily more united Europe seeking to establish a distinctive strategic policy to defend its interests will be obliged to consider some involvement in the tasks of containment of Soviet advances outside the NATO area?[13]

To complete this global strategic overview, the second hemisphere must be considered. To the west of the United States lie the Pacific Basin and South East Asia, beyond which the strategic hemispheres are reunited. The emergence of Japan as the most economically powerful nation in the region has already been remarked upon. The deployment of large and more capable Soviet forces in the area has increased the burdens of a policy of military containment in a region which the United States has traditionally regarded as its strategic backyard. Like Europe, the United States now faces a direct multi-dimensional threat to its own security, a threat which can only be countered by forward defence in both hemispheres.

This is the strategic background against which the statesmen of Europe will have to consider any plans for the future defence of the NATO area and for the contributions which their countries, so many of which have had proud national military traditions in the past, should make towards meeting the strategic objectives of the Western Alliance.

The Defence of NATO Area.

By definition, a triphibious strategy requires naval, land and air forces for its implementation. These forces have to be distributed over the NATO area to counter the diverse conventional military threats with which it is faced, and to maintain thereby the level of the nuclear threshold at an acceptable level. The increased range of offensive weapons and the mobility of the platforms from which they are launched (submarines, aircraft, ships, ground transporters) demand force deployments to provide forward and in depth defence wherever possible. Continuous surveillance of the perimeters of the NATO area by satellites and AWACS (the Airborne Warning and Control System already available to NATO) is essential, both to guard against strategic surprise and also, in conjunction with data from other intelligence sources, to ensure sufficient warning time to mobilise and deploy reserves and their equipment. It follows that at least a good proportion of these reserves should he kept at a higher degree of readiness than is the case at present.

How these forces are provided, by which allies, and in what proportions are the questions which lie at the heart of the problem of military burden-sharing within NATO. Acceptance of nuclear deterrence as the only effective means of preventing war in Europe points the way to a logical burden-sharing plan. The provision of such deterrence by Britain and France should be recognised as the first priority in their defence budgets, a priority which limits the amounts they can afford to spend on conventional arms, especially during periods when they are saddled with the costs of modernising their nuclear forces, as is the case at present.

Acceptance of the effectiveness of nuclear deterrence in Europe leads, as has been explained, to the valid assumption that a conventional Soviet assault against the Central Front is now less likely than it was in the early years of NATO and that the Soviets have more appealing strategic options to consider on a global basis than a "dash to the Rhine" or to the English Channel. Defence of the Central Front must no longer assume so totally dominant a place in NATO's strategic plans. They have to be replaced by a more realistic strategy which recognises that the defence of West German territory is only a part – indeed, still politically and militarily a crucially important part – of the defence of the NATO area as a whole.

The demands of a triphibious strategy to provide a conventional force shield for the NATO area and the composition and geo-political status of the European members of the Alliance suggest a natural division of military tasks with the "frontline" continental nations, giving priority to the defence of NATO'a land frontiers whilst those with maritime responsibilities do more for the defence of the ocean approaches to Europe and of its coastal waters. The United Kingdom is, of course, the outstanding example of an ally in the maritime category. Indeed, in any new plan for the defence of the NATO area, in which the European Allies play a more predominant role, agreement on a strategic principle to replace those which underpinned the commitments of the Brussels Treaty would be essential to the establishment of realistic burden-sharing.

The NATO Allies should agree once and for all that Britain's geography, history, military traditions, maritime expertise and the facts of her commercial life combine to make her a unique ally within NATO Europe, with national defence interests which differ from those of her continental neighbours, and with the latent ability to provide a distinctive contribution to the conventional defence of the NATO area.

After providing for the strategic nuclear deterrent force which is assigned to the Alliance, the United Kingdom's contribution to a triphibious strategy should reflect this distinctive capability. It should comprise maritime, air and rapid deployment forces (both amphibious and airborne) as well as forces to defend the British homeland, which is also NATO's most important forward base. But in addition, in order to provide some clear strategic linkage and as an evident assurance to its continental allies of Britain's commitment to NATO's overall deterrence and defence in Europe, the United Kingdom would retain a tactical air force and a reduced land force in the Federal Republic for as long as political considerations rendered their presence necessary.

The Defence of the Federal Republic of Germany. The Brussels Treaty Renewed.

A tripartite meeting of Britain, France and West Germany to prepare a new plan for the defence of the NATO area would signal the willingness of the three most militarily powerful nations in Western Europe to renew the provisions of the Brussels Treaty in a manner which would reflect the strategic realities of Europe on the eve of the Treaty's fortieth anniversary.

The question of the defence of West German territory – essentially the defence of the Central Front – is a nettle which European leaders have for too long been fearful to grasp. The reasons are not far to seek for, as Simpkin pointed out:

> *"The NATO centre provides an extreme and enduring example of the conflict between political, economic and cultural interests on the one hand, and military planning on the other."*[14]

A resolution of this conflict is now feasible. Acceptance of nuclear deterrence as the primary means of preventing war in Europe enables a new approach to be made to the problem of the conventional defence of this territory. With West German forces assuming responsibility for this conventional defence of the frontiers of the Federal Republic, and consequently for the maintenance of the nuclear threshold in that sector of the NATO perimeter, it will be possible to achieve a more realistic balance between the political and the military requirements for the continuing deployment of non-German forces within the Federal Republic.

The impact of new technology, more powerful conventional weapons for the land/air battle, and the evolution of tactical concepts to use these developments to the greatest advantage are combining to lessen the risks of numerical imbalance and even to allow some enhancement of the level of the nuclear threshold without the need for substantial increases in manpower. Discussing the growing importance of firepower through the ability of new weapons to discharge salvoes of undreamt of lethality, Simpkin forecast how:

> *"Large organised forces deployed at high density with a panoply of baroque equipment will become unusable in the very literal sense that they will be shot to pieces."*[15]

The balance of advantage on the battlefield is therefore tilting towards the defence. The utility of armoured vehicles in an offensive role is increasingly questioned owing to the their growing vulnerability to sophisticated mines, intelligent guided weapons, helicopters and air power of all kinds. The first charge on the West German defence budget should be the provision of a defensive shield of forces armed with these powerful new weapons and provided with ample air support.

United States land and air forces will remain in West Germany to provide the strategic linkage, referred to by M. Chirac in his speech to the WEU Assembly, which underwrites the United States nuclear guarantee to Europe. But the composition, role and deployment of these forces in the NATO defence plan can be reviewed in the light of the assumption by West Germany of the primary responsibility for the defence of its territory and the overall requirements of a triphibious strategy.

As neighbouring powers, and continental partners in NATO Europe, France, Belgium and the Netherlands should continue to maintain army units in Germany to preserve the present level of their contributions and to provide them with an element of forward defence of their own territories. In the case of France, the bilateral military agreements with West Germany compensate for France's continued reluctance to reassign her armed forces to the NATO military structure and assure as far as is politically possible the participation of the Rapid Action Force (FAR) in the event of an attack on Germany.

Britain's Army of the Rhine would be reduced in size. A self-contained force, equivalent to a division plus support (about 15,000 men), would be re-deployed west of the Rhine alongside the three clutch airfields of RAF

Germany. Initially, one of the armoured divisions of Rhine Army would have to be used to form this force, but in the longer term British policy should be to reduce the armoured component of her army and replace some tank regiments by mobile heli-troops equipped with a mix of attack and support helicopters (see Chaper VIII).

In the reorganisation of German forces to provide the forward defensive shield along the Central Front, the post of Commander-in-Chief, Northern Army Group would go to a German General in recognition of the assumption by West Germany of greater responsibility for the defence of its territory and of its willingness to take upon itself a more assertive role in the defence of Europe fully in keeping with its position as economically the strongest nation among the European members of NATO.

Here then is the basis of a plan for the defence of the Central Front in the context of a new triphibious strategy for the NATO area. It could lay the foundations for a European strategic structure based on a renewal of the Brussels Treaty which strengthened the European pillar of NATO.

The Maritime Dimension of NATO Strategy

The circumstances surrounding the founding of the North Atlantic Treaty made it inevitable that the defence of West Germany would become its primary strategic task and that, as a result, the whole character of NATO's structure and the ethos of its work would be predominantly military. At the time, an attack on West Germany by Soviet land and air forces was the only identifiable threat. The expansion of the Soviet Navy into a powerful ocean-going force had not yet begun and the Western Alliance enjoyed global maritime superiority. A year was to pass before NATO was given a maritime dimension by the appointment of a United States admiral as Supreme Allied Commander, Atlantic (SACLANT) with headquarters at Norfolk, Virginia, and wartime responsibilities for the security of the transatlantic reinforcement routes and for the conduct of offensive naval operations against enemy bases and in support of NATO forces in Europe.

Today, the maritime situation facing NATO is very different. The Soviet Northern Fleet, based around the vast complex of naval facilities in the Kola Peninsula, is the largest fleet in the Soviet navy with over half Russia's total of ballistic and cruise missile carrying nuclear submarines comprising its substantial underwater force. Its major surface combatants include an aircraft carrier, twelve cruisers, and thirty-six destroyers and frigates. A detachment is usually deployed in the Mediterranean. Naval aviation and amphibious shipping complete the fleet's main components.

In stark contrast, the European NATO navies and maritime air forces are generally smaller than they were even ten years ago. In particular, the Royal Navy, for long the backbone of NATO Europe's naval strength, has suffered the largest cut of all and, for the first time in living memory, its manpower is now slightly less than that of the French navy. There has also been a disastrous decline in the size of European merchant and deep sea fishing fleets and, in an emergency, a shortage of shipping would soon become apparent. The implications for wartime naval support and for the seaborne carriage of essential supplies are serious. Economic pressures, lack of competitiveness and the spread of the "short war" philosophy, inculcated by the growing acceptance of the inevitability of early nuclear retaliation in the event of war in Europe, have been the chief causes of these adverse maritime developments.

Beyond the NATO area, the former British naval presence has all but vanished, although a small force patrols the approaches to the Gulf to protect British shipping in the Iran/Iraq war zone. For her national needs, France maintains naval forces in the Indian Ocean and the Pacific; but the main task of maintaining the east-west strategic balance in these regions and providing a potential counter to Soviet naval activities falls to the hard pressed United States navy.

Overall, therefore, Western Europe finds itself in a position of serious maritime disadvantage, and a co-ordinated effort by the European Allies is needed to halt the decline in their naval capabilities. To counter the multi-dimensional threat, the forward defence of the NATO area must embrace its ocean approaches, coastal waters, offshore islands and installations, and the air space over them, in a huge arc from the North Cape to Gibraltar, including the whole European continental shelf. In the context of reliance upon nuclear deterrence to prevent war, the provision of these forces – the maritime and maritime air components of the triphibious strategy – is just as important, in some ways more important, than the provision of a conventional shield along the central front. These outer fringes of the NATO area are those where the risks of a Soviet attempt to test the credibility of NATO's nuclear deterrent are greater than in the centre and the dangers to NATO's strategic real estate more evident.

The maritime defence of Western Europe is a European responsibility in peace time and it is high time that the Allied political leaders recognised this fact. Apart from the Sixth Fleet in the Mediterranean, the United States maintains no standing naval deployment in European waters in peacetime. Why should she? Her increased strategic responsibilities now cast some doubts over the likelihood of the timely arrival of the Carrier Battle Groups, which form the United States Strike Fleet into the NATO area in an emergency. This is the only naval force assigned to NATO which is capable of dealing with the Soviet Northern Fleet and covering the passage of seaborne reinforcements to defend Norway or prevent the occupation of Iceland.

As always, the problem is financial. The provision of sophisticated, technically advanced and highly capable naval and maritime air forces is very expensive. Within the Western Alliance, only the USA can afford to maintain the full range of such forces. It would be unrealistic to suggest that the

European Allies should seek to emulate this capability even as part of any European defence grouping. However, these allies must act soon to organise their existing and still not inconsiderable naval and maritime air forces into a more co-ordinated body with defined responsibilities for the maritime defence of the NATO area and for maintaining a viable level of nuclear threshold in the maritime sphere. The importance of a high degree of interoperability between units of different nations, achieved by standardisation of equipment and tactical procedures, cannot be over-emphasised.

Above all, any further rundown of European maritime assets must be avoided. Nowhere is this essential step more necessary than in the United Kingdom. The need for allied agreement on the unique strategic and military status of Britain and on the importance to NATO of her remaining the foremost European maritime power, has already been pointed out. (See page 107.) The opinion of one of Britain's most respected commentators on naval affairs supports the case for this realignment in British defence policy and for the recasting of Britain's contribution to NATO which it would entail:

> *"A case thus exists, on both political and strategic grounds, for arguing that the British contribution to NATO should progressively be realigned away from territorial defence of the Central Front towards air and naval defence of maritime communications and, with military assistance, the defence of Norway and the islands of the North Atlantic. This would be a major change in British defence policy with repercussions far beyond the future of the Navy."*[16]

The decision of the British government announced in December 1986, to retain an amphibious force and assault ships was a welcome sign that at least the case for this change had not been totally rejected.

Two further points need to be made. Britain and France are the only two NATO nations possessing balanced multi-role navies, with their own organic air power and afloat support, which are capable of prolonged overseas deployments and power projection outside the NATO area. In the foreseeable future, no other European ally is likely to acquire a similar maritime capability. In considering the need for European participation in the defence of vital Western interests overseas, this fact should not be forgotten. It is another reason why the declining trend of British naval power should be halted and reversed.

Finally, it is clear that the defence of the NATO perimeter requires larger naval forces than are currently available. Spain is a source from which such reinforcements could be obtained. It is in the military interests of the Western Alliance that Spain should join the integrated command structure of NATO and assign her armed forces to the Alliance at the earliest opportunity. "*A la Carte*" membership of NATO is no substitute for the commitment of national forces to the common cause which the present strategic situation demands.

Air Power. Vital Partner and Third Force.

By now it should have become clear to the reader that the concept of air power as a medium for the employment of armed forces separate from and independent of sea power and land armies has been much weakened by the entry into service of ballistic missile systems and by the development of operational doctrines and tactical procedures in which aircraft, fixed wing and rotary, are an essential component of forces deployed at sea or on land. Although a triphibious strategy implies, by definition, the existing need for three separate components of military power – at sea, on land, and in the air – for its implementation, nevertheless, for the purposes of this study, such a treatment of air power on its own is more a reflection of the in way which a nation's armed forces are structured and administered than of modern fighting methods.

A separate air force, as a third armed service, is still the most usual and appropriate means of providing, organising, and accounting for the military aircraft of all varieties and types which a nation's defence commitments require. The extent to which navies and armies are allowed to own and operate their own aircraft is often a source of inter-service rivalry which sometimes prejudices operational efficiency (an example is the clumsy arrangements for the control of British battlefield helicopters which is divided between the Army and the Royal Air Force). An exception of almost universal application is the now generally accepted principle that navies own and operate aircraft which are embarked in warships. In Italy, however, mindful of air force objections, the government is reluctant to enact legislation which would allow the navy to operate fixed-wing aircraft in its new aircraft carrier. Furthermore, in the case of shore-based maritime patrol aircraft there are differences in the arrangements for their ownership and control amongst the NATO European allies; for some are an air force and others a naval responsibility.

However aircraft are operated or controlled, the objective of air power in the defence of the NATO area is to maintain control of the air space above the area and beyond it (to the limits at which stand off weapons or cruise missiles can be launched) in order to protect naval forces at sea, armies on the ground, and national territories and assets from attack by air launched weapons of whatever type. This clearly includes the need for offensive counter-air operations.

For the rest, the problems of providing adequate numbers of aircraft for the defence of Europe are broadly similar to those encountered in the provision of maritime forces, notably cost, the need for standardisation of types and interoperability, and above all of international collaboration in the design, development and production of fixed wing aircraft and helicopters. By the mid-eighties, there was progress on all these fronts.

One potential source of increased air power, however, appears to be neglected. National arrangements for the earmarking of civil air liners and helicopters for rapid conversion to military use in an emergency are often inadequate and sometimes virtually non-existent. In the context of a "short war" this could be a dangerous oversight, as is the lack of any reserve flying squadrons in the Royal Air Force in Britain and in most other West European countries, unlike the United States.

CHAPTER VIII

A British Defence Policy for the Twenty-first Century

The Political and Strategic Background

THE United Kingdom's present contribution of both nuclear and conventional deterrent forces to NATO was begun when the illusion that the post-war British economy could support the military trappings of great power status prevailed. The reality of the state of relative penury which had resulted from our stupendous war effort and the decline in our economic status had not yet been fully understood. After twenty years of defence "reviews", cutting of military commitments, salami slicing of equipment programmes and continuous reductions in manpower, this illusion still clouds the decision making process in the formulation of British defence policy. What else can account for the belief that the level of national resources which even a Conservative government supposedly supportive of national security issues was ready to provide would be sufficient to pay for the twenty-year Trident programme of modernisation of the strategic nuclear deterrent force and for the even more expensive re-equipment programme for the conventional forces which would necessarily coincide with it?

The level of resources devoted to national security is indeed the nub of the matter. In the post-war years the international status of the United Kingdom has been transformed. From being one of the "Big Three" great powers it has become merely one of the three most important medium powers in Western Europe, a very different situation. Furthermore, this status now depends principally upon its military capabilities, particularly on the possession of nuclear weapons. The inherent weaknesses of the post-war British economy are unlikely ever to enable Britain to maintain its international status by financial strength alone.

No responsible British government should connive either knowingly or by default at any further erosion of the United Kingdom's position in the world. Indeed there is no evident public demand for such an erosion to take place or for the country to become less important or influential, although, to be fair, the question of making sacrifices in the national interest has received little public discussion. The position has now been reached when a responsible government will have to answer this question on the public's behalf and explain the reasons for the nature of its reply.

To maintain in the future a credible nuclear deterrent force and conventional forces capable of making a contribution to the defence of the NATO area, appropriate to one of the most militarily powerful European members of NATO and adequate to cope with the direct defence of the country and of its remaining overseas interests, will require higher levels of defence spending than those authorised by the Conservative Government in the years after 1985 (see page 25). By then it was clear that without major changes in economic and particularly in social policies, a peak had been reached in the scale of resources devoted to defence which any future government, whatever its political persuasion, would be able to provide. Welfare would have finally won its prolonged struggle over weapons. But would this victory reflect the true wishes of the British people or indeed be in their best interests in the long term?

The reality is stark. As the costs of the equipment programmes rose ministerial illusions were gradually shattered. The clear but unstated object of the 1981 Defence Review ("The Way Forward") was to reduce the size of the conventional forces to a level and to equip them to a scale which could be afforded during the twenty-year life of the Trident programme and during a period when the costs of new weapons and of new equipment would rise well above the rate of national inflation.

Other measures, designed to mitigate the worst effects of the review, but which contributed eventually to the present situation, were also introduced. To improve the "teeth to tail" ratios of all the services, the cut of 11,000 in naval manpower has been applied in shore postings as far as possible, the Army has redeployed three per cent of its manpower from support areas to the front line, and in the Royal Air Force there will be a fifteen per cent increase in front-line aircraft strength without any increase in uniformed manpower.[1]

Nevertheless, necessary though many of these measures undoubtedly were, as were those to improve procurement procedures and to introduce competitive tendering (the fundamental reorganisation of the Royal Dockyards, in particular, was long overdue), their net effect has been to scrape clean every barrel of economy and cost-effectiveness. Little or no administrative fat now remains to be slimmed from the body of the British Armed Forces, rather the reverse. Signs of "overstretch" are already appearing. Some recruitment targets are proving difficult to fill. Levels of manpower retention are causing concern. In short, British defence policy is stuck against the buffers of political temerity, administrative inertia and insufficient resources.

By the time of the General Election, Britain's conventional forces will have been cut to a level which prejudices the country's ability to maintain the present multi-role contribution to the defence of the NATO area including the direct defence of the United Kingdom and its overseas interests against threats ranging from low intensity peacetime campaigns to full scale war. The unenviable but inevitable choice facing a future British government is either to increase defence spending or to maintain it at the levels of the mid-eighties and in so doing accept a further diminution of the country's status within the Western Alliance.

Ever since the 1981 review, British ministers have steadfastly maintained that:

> *"The resources which can realistically be postulated for defence in the longer term are sufficient to sustain these roles and to provide for the major re-equipment programmes of the services currently foreseen."*[2]

Summarising his evidence to the Commons Defence Committee in its examination of the 1986 Defence Statement, George Younger, the Secretary of State, repeated this assurance:

> *"My judgment is that although there will be some difficult decisions to marry up the resources in the budget to our commitments, there will be no question of having to withdraw from any major commitment or any major part thereof."*[3]

TABLE 8.1
BRITAIN'S DEFENCE BUDGET
1986–87

		£Million	Percentage
Total Expenditure		18,479	100.0
Strategic Nuclear Deterrent Force		658	3.6
Defence of the United Kingdom		2,045	11.0
Defence of NATO Central Front		3,499	18.9
BAOR including reinforcements	2,550		
RAF Germany including reinforcements	897		
Berlin Garrison	52		
Maritime Operations		3,170	17.1
Eastern Atlantic	2,618		
Channel	552		
Amphibious and Mobile Forces		420	2.3
Amphibious Capability	115		
Allied Cmnd Europe Mobile Force	38		
UK Mobile Force	267		
Out of Area Commitments (Falklands, Belize, Hong Kong, Cyprus, Brunei, Gibraltar)		554	3.0
Research & Development		2,327	12.6
Training		1,257	6.8
Equipment Support & Associated Facilities in UK		983	5.3
War & Contingency Stocks		405	2.2
Other Support Functions		3,184	17.2
Miscellaneous Expenditure & Receipts		–23	
	TOTAL	18,479	100.0

Sources: 1. SDE 86 Table 2.5.
2. House of Commons. Second Report from the Defence Committee Session 1985–86. Statement on Defence Estimates 1986 p.136.

Nevertheless, in the context of Britain's future role in NATO, talk of withdrawal from a major commitment is inappropriate and unnecessarily alarming to her allies. What ministers – indeed the whole British Cabinet – now have to grasp, is the urgent need to establish a national approach to the major strategic problems that are developing within NATO, namely the emerging evolution of political initiatives for the establishment of a more closely co-ordinated European defence policy, possibly leading to the formation of a European strategic group, the need for a new triphibious strategy for the defence of the NATO area, and the role that Britain is best suited to play in the implementation of such a strategy. In defining this role, the policy of the 4 Cs (see page 16) remains valid in principle, but drastic revision of the manner of its application will be necessary, especially the linkages between national defence needs and the national contribution to NATO's collective defence.

Britain's New Role in Alliance Defence

In the discussions on these issues, which will soon be necessary if French initiatives in WEU and between Paris and Bonn are to be followed up, the United Kingdom should table proposals for a British military role which will ensure her status as a major European power but be within a realistic assessment of her future economic potential to provide. This role should recognise that the provision of a strategic nuclear deterrent force is Britain's principal contribution to the maintenance of peace in Europe. In addition it should include a substantial contribution to the triphibious conventional strategy for the defence of the NATO area. This latter contribution will reflect the country's unique position amongst the Continental Allies and her natural suitability to play a distinctive part in the collective defence of Western Europe and of its overseas interests (*see Table 8.2 Britain's Strategic Tasks for the 1990s*).

This distinctive role should combine national and NATO defence needs wherever possible. A widening of ministerial strategic horizons will be necessary in Britain. The oft-repeated shibboleth that "*the forward defence of the Federal Republic is the forward defence of Britain itself*"[4] will have to be revised. In the context of an allround defence of the NATO area, it is only a part of Britain's forward defence, but a principal component of the defence of West German territory for which the Federal Republic should assume the chief responsibility. The Brussels Treaty commitments have been overtaken by political and strategic developments, and need to be modified.

Also in this context of comprehensive allround forward defence, the security of the North West Approaches to Europe and of Norway are equally important; guaranteeing both should be regarded as a priority task for the United Kingdom. Any realistic assessment of the multi-dimensional

TABLE 8.2
BRITAIN'S STRATEGIC TASKS FOR THE 1990s
(Listed in order of priority for resource allocation)

National Defence	Contribution to the Defence of the NATO Area or of NATO Interests	Forces Required
A. *Nuclear* 1. *Provision of Strategic Nuclear Deterrent Force*	= Strategic Nuclear Deterrent Force Assigned to NATO (Principal Role)	Trident SLBM Force
B. *Conventional* 1(a) *Forward Defence of the United Kingdom* North East Atlantic Western Approaches and Overhead Air Space	= Forward Defence of NATO's UK Base and of N.W. Perimeter of NATO Area. (Principal conventional role)	AWACS and satellite surveillance, offensive support aircraft Major surface warships and embarked aircraft Amphibious shipping and forces Air Support Ships Afloat support Nuclear & conventional fleet submarines Maritime Patrol Aircraft Extended air defence forces Rapid intervention land forces
B. 1(b) *Close-in & Direct Defence of the UK*	= Close-in and direct defence of NATO's UK base (Principal conventional role)	Integrated Air Defence & Anti-Missile Systems Flexible & mobile land forces Offshore patrol vessels, other minor war vessels, mine warfare forces, Medium-range maritime patrol aircraft & helicopters Skeleton Civil Defence organisation
B. 2. *Forward Defence of the UK* Provision of strategic linkage with Europe by limited land/air presence in West Germany	= Forward Defence of NATO's UK Base through contribution to direct defence of West German territory (secondary conventional role)	Tactical Air Force Self-contained mobile land force of divisional strength
B. 3. *Defence of National Interests Overseas* Deployment as required of forces in B.1(a) above, and, if needed, of forces in B.2 above	= Unique (except for France) capability to deploy flexible & mobile forces as contribution to defence of NATO European interests outside the NATO area (Secondary conventional role)	As in B.1(a) above

threat to the NATO area and of the need to maintain the nuclear threshold should recognise that the defence of these areas is both the forward defence of the United Kingdom and also the defence in depth of the Federal Republic.

In a similar perspective the national duty of any British government to defend the realm, in this case the territory, air space, and coastal waters of the British Isles, represents a vital contribution to the defence of the NATO area since it provides also for the defence of the Alliance's principal forward base in Europe. In view of the direct threat to national territories of all the European allies that improved Soviet military capabilities have created, more attention has to be given to the defence of these territories within the overall strategic plan.

The Cardinal Points of a NEW British Defence Policy

> *"A new defence policy is needed, which will exploit all the developing techniques of mobility and firepower to achieve deliberate and sane objectives. It will probably need a great general staff and powerful political leadership to work it out and sustain it. At the moment there is no sign of either."* ("*The Meaning of Thorneycroft*", by Leonard Beaton. *The Statist*, London, 24 Aug. 1962)

In 1962 this prescription for a new British defence policy may have seemed to be ahead of its time. A quarter of a century later, it describes with extraordinary accuracy the basis on which such a policy should be drawn up. The important changes in the country's higher organisation for defence introduced by Michael Heseltine on New Year's Day, 1985, have provided a unified and integrated military/civilian Defence Policy and Operational Staff within the Ministry of Defence which should prove fully capable of grasping the tremendous problems involved in preparing the new policy and solving them in a realistic and forward-looking manner. What remains an unknown quantity is the degree of political impetus which will be mobilised for this essential task. Strong political leadership will certainly be needed to bring the policy to fruition.

A new strategic role for Britain in the Western Alliance has been proposed. What are the cardinal points of the programme required to combine national and Alliance security needs in the most cost effective and constructive manner? Before embarking on a more detailed discussion of these points, it is necessary to put forward a new approach to defence policy which any future British government should adopt in the national interest.

A defence policy designed to assist to the greatest possible extent in the attainment of other national objectives set by governments (in the circumstances of Britain in the eighties these are most likely to be industrial and social objectives) should be one of the first considerations of those entrusted with the task of its preparation, provided always that the principle that defence requirements are paramount and cannot be subordinated to any political expediency is maintained.[5]

As *The Times* pointed out when discussing the implications of the disastrous Nimrod AEW fiasco:

> *"The Westland crisis, which exposed fatuous Whitehall jealousies over responsibilities for different companies, stemmed from a sudden lack of British government orders. The needs of industry were ignored in juggling with figures for the defence budget. That process is now damaging Britain's warship building industry."*[6]

The lack of orders for military helicopters which created the fatal gap in the Westland order book was mainly due to the failure of the Ministry of Defence to agree on the future helicopter needs of the Army, a matter which had been under discussion for more than a year, and in so doing to resolve the squabbles between the Army and the Royal Air Force over the division of responsibilities for the provision, control and operation of battlefield helicopters.

The effect on the industry's labour force of delays in the placing of warship orders imposed by the Defence Ministry for budgetary control reasons has already been mentioned. Improved co-operation between the government departments concerned and some relaxation of the rigid rules for the switching of funds between them in cases where the national interest would benefit, are needed to improve this situation and to enable defence policy to contribute more to the overall aims of government.

Forces Manpower

Plans for the provision of a cheaper source of manpower for the Armed Forces to augment a smaller cadre of professional long-service regulars should be drawn up. In so doing, ways should be sought to make the greatest possible impact on the social and employment objectives of improving youth training, increasing youth employment, and providing opportunities for wider public participation in the defence of the realm.

The reintroduction of military National Service in Britain would achieve all these objectives and provide as well a steady flow of trained reserves, the other component of military manpower which the nation so evidently lacks. No other decision by a British government could do more to end the uncertain notes over the future course of United Kingdom defence and strategic policy which have emanated from Whitehall and the Westminster trumpets for so long. The determination of Britain to remain one of the most powerful military powers in Western Europe would be made manifest to her allies, as would her desire to restore a sense of patriotism and an understanding of the responsibilities of citizenship be made clear to her people.

If the political will to reintroduce military national service in Britain is lacking, then other means of recruiting for short-term engagements will have to be introduced, but whatever method is chosen there will be fewer long-service regulars. And if the fatal combination of political temerity and bureaucratic inertia fails to confront the problem of British forces manpower, those forces will become smaller for the simple reason that the defence budget will no longer be able to accommodate the present levels of expensive regular manpower without unacceptable cuts in the equipment budget.

Inevitably, therefore, the present organisation, composition and functions of Britain's regular forces will require a searching review. This review should address itself to two fundamental questions both demanding early attention, namely the manpower structure and the complex "quality versus quantity" argument when considering the future provision not only of weapons, platforms and equipment, but of skilled and unskilled personnel as well.

In both these questions similar factors will figure prominently, notably demographic trends, social and educational change, technological advances, particularly in the development of sophisticated command and control systems, and the growing diversity of threats to both national and Alliance security, including those at the lower end of the intensity spectrum, with which the military are likely to have to deal even during a further period of "peace". Never absent from any discussion will be the heavy hand of the Treasury, seeking to restrain the enthusiasms of the military planners with dire warnings of the limited financial resources likely to be available for future defence budgets.

In the quarter of a century since the ending of National Service in Britain, the traditional military structure of commissioned officers, non-commissioned officers (Chief and Petty Officers in the Royal Navy) and other ranks has reached a stage where major alterations are needed to adapt it to the demands of the future. In particular the duties and responsibilities of both commissioned and non-commissioned officers have to be reassessed and new establishment scales drawn up to provide the subtle mixture of military command and civilian management skills which is now essential for the maintenance of efficient and cost-effective armed forces.

Today, Britain has too many commissioned officers particularly in the middle ranks (Lieut-Colonel to Major General and equivalents in the RN and the RAF), and a corpus of non-commissioned officers broadly sufficient in numbers but deprived of many opportunities to exercise fully those aspects of middle management for which it is well trained. In short there is insufficient delegation of command and responsibility.

Comparisons with the armed forces of other nations are revealing. The British and French navies, for example, have similar manpower totals, yet the French Navy has some 4,000 fewer officers than the Royal Navy. In the case of land forces, as Simpkin points out, combat units of the German army have always had a smaller establishment of officers than their British counterparts. He compares the twenty officers of a 1944 German tank battalion with the thirty-six in a British armoured regiment today with the same number of tanks.[7] The Royal Air Force has the lowest officer to man ratio of the three services and its officer establishment appears excessive in relation to its total front-line aircraft strength. This reflects the need to compete with the civilian economy for expensive technically qualified manpower.

New patterns of engagement and service are needed for future commissioned officer recruitment. There should be fewer of them than now but their education and training should be as good as, if not better, than that available to entrants to the civilian professions. Instead of the traditional offer of what is virtually a lifetime career from eighteen to the mid fifties, aspiring officers should be entered for a shorter term, say one of twenty years from age eighteen, on an engagement which offers reasonable prospects of achieving a command appointment, highly selective opportunities for those considered suitable for the higher ranks of each Service to extend their service for a full career, and for those who leave earlier, a transferable or portable pension, with the opportunity of really worthwhile service on the Reserves, such as a flying appointment with the Royal Auxilliary Air Force.

These arrangements would accommodate the effects of the blustery winds of change which seem likely to blow through British employment practices, namely greater occupational mobility, two, perhaps three, careers in a working life, periods of self-employment and portable personal pensions. They would recognise that fighting in the front-line operational conditions of a future war has become an activity of such relentless tempo and extreme intensity that only those under the age of forty-five at most, will be able to stand the pace. A corps of officers engaged to serve to an age beyond which their operational usefulness in active war would be waning but which would not be too late for the development of a successful second career (for which experience of military command would often be an invaluable asset) would suit the much needed changes in British employment practice.

Quality versus Quantity

Sophisticated, advanced, high performance platforms, weapons and electronic control systems for the deployment of air and maritime power have become the most expensive items in a nation's conventional armoury. The present situation of Britain's Royal Air Force provides an interesting example of the consequences of the single-minded pursuit of quality both in men and in material in the provision of military air power.

On completion of the RAF's current re-equipment programme, over half of Britain's front line combat aircraft strength will be represented by the 220 Tornado GR1 strike-attack and the 165 Tornado F2 (the air defence variant) aircraft. With the unit cost of each aircraft now standing at over £17 million, the total cost will eventually be more than that of re-equipping Britain's strategic nuclear deterrent force with the Trident SLBM system. The enormous costs of the Tornado programme, vital as it is, inhibit the provision of other types of aircraft and helicopters, particularly those for maritime tasks and Army support, and prevent the establishment of any reserve flying squadrons and their equipment with less expensive, but nevertheless useful, aircraft capable of reinforcing the country's military air power in an emergency.

With air force manpower it is the same story. The Royal Air Force has a total strength of 93,400 regulars to operate, maintain and administer its establishment of some 635 combat aircraft. By way of contrast the Israeli air force with a combat strength of 629 aircraft (of which ninety may be stored) numbers 28,000 in peacetime.[8] The national circumstances and the security problems of the two countries are totally different but the difference in their respective manpower to aircraft ratios is too wide for any British complacency. It strengthens the impression that the Royal Air Force is somewhat extravagantly managed; Heseltine's attempt to improve its "teeth to tail" ratio evidently did not go far enough.

Britain's air force policy of expensive front-line quality both in men and material unsupported by any reserve flying units is strategically dangerous (another example of the "short war" philosophy) and absorbs too great a proportion of the defence budget in relation to what it provides in terms of input to the country's overall military capabilities. The future provision of British airpower should be based on a more cost-effective combination of high performance aircraft, including those specialised for maritime tasks and for support of the land battle, and more numerous, less expensive, aircraft manned by reservists who are frequently exercised and kept at a state of readiness compatible with NATO's mobilisation plans.

In the manpower cuts imposed by the 1981 defence review (Cmnd. 8288 – The Way Forward) the Royal Navy was by far the worst sufferer. Yet despite these cuts, only slightly alleviated by post Falklands policy adjustments, it has succeeded in maintaining an operational fleet of almost exactly the same size and composition as that which existed before "The Way Forward" was published.

Although naval manpower policy has never been extravagant, it has now become necessary to improve the sea–shore service ratio still further, to the point where the retention of valuable trained men is beginning to suffer. As to naval reserves, the volunteer Royal Naval Reserve (RNR) is an active seagoing force equipped with modern vessels for its vital wartime task of minesweeping and mine counter-measures work.

The Royal Navy has followed a policy of acquiring quality assets for its surface and submarine fleets rather than one of quantity, which larger numbers of less capable (and cheaper) units would provide. In practice, no other choice has been open to it. For over twenty years successive governments have mined and sapped into British naval strength. The 1966, 1975 and 1981 Defence Reviews were the markers on this short-sighted and ill-advised course.

The Royal Navy could only respond by devoting the bulk of its resources to the struggle of maintaining the core units of a balanced, ocean-going fleet, self-sufficient in air and afloat support, which is still essential to an island nation obliged to exercise maritime power in the defence of its territory and interests, and to make a major naval contribution to the security of the NATO Alliance. The bottom line in British naval strength has now been reached. Any further reduction in the country's maritime assets, whether naval, commercial, trained manpower or shipbuilding capacity, will dangerously prejudice national security, a point of which by the end of 1986 one or two government ministers had become dimly aware.

With this partially successful struggle now behind it, the Royal Navy should adjust its quality–quantity ratio by accepting that, provided they are equipped with close-in defences to deal with a defined, if limited, threat, cheaper, simpler and possibly somewhat slower surface hull platforms can provide a cost-effective means of multiplying the amount of maritime power that a medium-sized nation can realistically deploy.

The concept of the aviation support ship, a merchant type hull equipped to house, maintain and operate an embarked force of a mix of Sea Harrier VSTOL aircraft and anti-submarine helicopters, is a classic example of such a force multiplier. In company with a quality unit, such as an "*Invincible*" class small aircraft carrier, capable of tasking and controlling the support ship's aircraft, it would greatly increase the ASW and in-depth defence capabilities of a surface task or convoy escort force.

A similar approach should be examined when deciding on the replacement of at least one of the Royal Navy's two ageing assault ships, "*Intrepid*" and "*Fearless*". Lower down the scale, a new class of Offshore Patrol Vessel (OPV), carrying a helicopter and equipped with anti-submarine weapons and sensors, could usefully combine the peacetime performance of those constabulary duties of fishery protection and patrol of the enlarged economic zone (EEZ) to which the Royal Navy has been obliged to give a low priority in its total pursuit of quality, with the important wartime role of the defence of coastal and inshore waters.

The Reserve Forces

A credible European nuclear deterrent may lessen the likelihood of a Warsaw Pact attack on the central front, but it does not permit any further reduction of the conventional defences of the NATO area against the Soviet multi-dimensional threat. An ubiquitous nuclear threshold has to be maintained. Since, to some extent, economic factors but, above all, lack of political will, limit the amount of conventional military strength that Western Europe is ready to deploy permanently in peacetime, advantage must be taken of the increased warning time provided by advanced surveillance systems to keep reserve forces and the stockpiles of weapons and equipment which they will require on mobilisation at the highest possible state of readiness.

In Britain, whether or not National Service is restored, the existing volunteer reserve forces should be retained and enlarged to provide the widest possible range of military skills. There are many civilians whose training, employment, or even leisure pursuits make them immediately useful to the armed forces in an emergency. They should be encouraged to join the volunteer reserve forces and become, in the words of Sir Winston Churchill, "*twice a citizen*".

In some categories more positive means of ensuring that essential skills are available for national needs in wartime are necessary anyway. For example, the recruitment of civil airline pilots, both rotary and fixed-wing, could greatly assist the establishment of operational flying squadrons in the Royal Auxiliary Air Force, the lack of which remains one of the most glaring deficiencies of Britain's present reserve system.

Flexibility, Mobility, Firepower

Flexibility, mobility and firepower should be the hallmarks of Britain's armed forces in future. Flexibility is the capacity of a fighting unit to perform military tasks in differing geographical areas and in varying climatic conditions without the need for major changes in equipment, weapons, stores or personnel. The majority of major warships, military aircraft and helicopters are inherently flexible. In the case of land forces, the infantry regiment is extremely flexible, an armoured regiment of main battle tanks is by comparison inflexible. For a medium power, such as Britain, with varying military commitments and limited financial resources to meet them, it is clearly more cost-effective to possess armed forces of maximum flexibility.

There are two aspects of mobility, strategic and tactical. Naval and air forces are inherently mobile on both counts. The techniques of replenishment at sea have raised the mobility of naval surface forces to the point where they can now deploy and operate far from base for weeks on end. They, therefore, possess complete strategic and tactical mobility and are virtually immune from the threat of diplomatic or political opposition.

Whilst in-flight refuelling has improved the tactical mobility of shore-based and Naval aircraft and increased their endurance, the strategic mobility of air forces can still be limited by the availability of bases and, on occasion, as the United States Air Force was made painfully aware during the operations against Libya in April 1986, by political refusal of clearance to allow over-flying of national territories or entry into national air-space.

The scale of battlefield mobility ranges between the infantryman on Shanks' pony and the assault or support helicopter. Somewhere in between comes the main battle tank. Over and above its very limited tactical mobility and its increasing vulnerability to both air and surface launched weapons, its greatest disadvantage – which makes it less suitable for the British Army than for continental land forces – is its lack of strategic mobility and flexibility. The only aircraft in the NATO inventory capable of carrying a main battle tank is the United States C-5A Galaxy and only sixty-five of them exist.

Effectively, therefore, Britain's armoured forces which comprise around twenty per cent of its army's combat strength would be anchored in war to the sixty-five kilometre sector of the Central Front for which the British Army of the Rhine is at present responsible. If threats develop elsewhere there would be no means of moving them. As to flexibility, main battle tanks are all but useless in the countless small local wars, peace-keeping duties and counter-insurgency operations in which the British Army has been engaged almost continuously since the end of World War II. Although a falling incidence of these activities may now seem likely, they could well be replaced by more frequent and more widespread low-intensity threats to the peaceful existence of British citizens. The civil power may require military assistance in dealing with these threats. Tanks have played no part in the long-drawn campaign against terrorism in Northern Ireland.

In the new role proposed for Britain in a triphibious strategy for the defence of the NATO area, land forces possessing the maximum possible degree of flexibility and mobility will be needed. In the long term the armoured component of the British Army's combat strength should be reorganised on the lines of France's Force d'Action Rapide (see Table 7.2) to comprise air portable armoured vehicles and personnel carriers and larger numbers of helicopters than are at present possessed by the Army of the Rhine.

Whilst this transformation would represent a major and no doubt controversial change in the Army's structure and organisation, nevertheless it would provide Britain with the more strategically flexible and tactically mobile land forces that it will require in the future. The whole combat strength of the Army would then have a multi-role capability, as able to operate in any sector of the European front, flanks or centre, as to deploy rapidly out of area in the defence of national or Alliance interests. All combat formations would also be able to contribute to the direct defence of the United Kingdom and to provide assistance to the civil power when needed. It goes without saying that an essential prerequisite to such a reorganisation would be the transfer of responsibility for all battlefield helicopters, whatever their role, from the Royal Air Force to the Army, and the establishment of command procedures for their operational use similar to the naval policy in which helicopters form an integral part of the weapons systems of the force in which they are embarked.

There is another reason for allotting a larger role to the helicopter in the Army's order of battle which is relevant to the need for readily available reserves and equipment able to become operational within the likely NATO mobilisation period. In Britain today there are over five hundred helicopters in civil use and some 350 of these are civil versions of military types, such as Sea Kings and Pumas. Many of these civil helicopter pilots have had previous flying experience in the Armed Forces. With the provision of rapid conversion weapon and equipment kits, this civil helicopter force represents a source of readily available "force multipliers" to augment the rotary wing forces not only of the Army but of the other services as well, just as air-liners, merchant ships and heavy goods vehicles will be requisitioned in an emergency.

The firepower of many existing and projected weapons systems is unprecedented (see page 108). Britain's forces must be equipped to reap the full benefits of such developments as "fire and forget" guided weapons which, amongst other and similar new arrivals, will cause major changes in the nature of land warfare, and will swing the battlefield balance more in favour of effective defence. Stressing the desirability of European participation in the SDI research programme, the London *Times* pointed out how, as the programme progressed:

> *"The focus will then shift from the technicalities of space-based missile defence to the land and air battle in Europe. Here colossal defensive advantages can now be achieved . . . through the impact of its superior technology the West is now confronted with an opportunity to achieve a reduction in strategic and tactical vulnerability which has been inconceivable for most of the last forty years."* [9]

Continental or Maritime? No Need for Further Strategic Argument

Throughout the post-war period inter-service rivalries, arguments and jealousies have frequently prejudiced the quality of professional advice given to ministers attempting the difficult, and sometimes impossible, task of determining priorities in the allocation of financial resources which were never sufficient for military demands and often in actual decline. Conversely, there have been occasions when, losing patience with the advice they were receiving, ministers have taken matters into their own hands and produced their own policies, on some occasions with a minimum of prior discussion (the Heseltine reform of the higher levels of the Ministry of Defence) and on others against the advice they were receiving from at least some members of their staffs (the 1981 Defence Review).

The strategic circumstances which led to the formation of NATO and the subsequent British undertaking to maintain 55,000 troops and a tactical air force permanently in West Germany have combined to exacerbate the imbalance in the structure of Britain's armed forces and the long-running argument as to whether priority in British defence resource allocation should be given to the pursuance of a "continental" or a "maritime" strategy. The steadfast determination of successive British governments to adhere to the Brussels Treaty commitments despite the enormous political, strategic and economic changes which have taken place, both nationally and within the Western Alliance, have added fuel to the flames of inter-service argument. As a defence academic explained:

> *"NATO was the lever which enabled the Army to usurp the Navy's position in popular and budgetary priorities . . . The Royal Navy was, therefore, caricatured as the imperial legacy of a once great power. The evidence of both world wars was used to demonstrate that Britain was inextricably bound to the continental land mass and that since 1945 she had – albeit reluctantly – begun to acknowledge this in her strategy."* [10]

In the past two decades the advance of technology and its application to the conduct of war, and the fundamental changes in the military threats now facing NATO Europe, have relegated to the history books this traditional argument over British strategic policy. In the concept of a triphibious strategy for the forward and in-depth defence of the NATO area in which sea, land and air forces each have their part to play, more often acting together than separately, there is no strategic choice for Britain to make nor any cause for further inter-Service arguments and rivalries. Both in the proposed British contribution to this strategy and in meeting the demands of national security at home or overseas, there will be ample and rewarding work for all three Services to perform. The Conservative Government has already set the scene for the future:

> *"The Government is determined to uphold the leadership, loyalties and traditions which are essential to the morale of the individual services and their fighting capability. This country's experience of modern warfare, most recently in the Falklands campaign, has progressively demonstrated, however, the need for the Services to be equipped and trained to fight together."* [11]

CHAPTER IX

CONCLUSION

If poverty exists in Britain it is a poverty largely of expectations – a dull, fatalistic mediocre belief that nothing will change, that no serious effort for improvement is worthwhile, a disinterested and resigned acceptance of tawdry material circumstances and national decline. In the field of security policy and national defence complacency about the Soviet threat is rife in Parliament, in the media, among the general public and even in the Services themselves. The Armed Forces reflect the relative economic decline of the nation and also its moral and intellectual impoverishment, characterised by lack of original ideas, a paucity of confident radical thinking, of bold innovation and dynamic leadership.

Even an operation like the Falklands War would be difficult to mount today, so great is the scarcity of merchant shipping. The Air Defence of Britain would be severely strained by a major Soviet air attack on the United Kingdom owing to the inadequacy of the Airborne Early Warning available, caused by the Nimrod Mk.3 fiasco, the lack of fighter aircraft and the deficiencies of the Tornado F3 radar. At sea, the reinforcement of North West Europe would be perilous indeed for lack of escort vessels in face of a formidable Soviet submarine threat. On the Central Front, the position in peacetime looks more secure, but the flower of Britain's professional Army is exposed and irrecoverable in the Federal Republic of Germany, vulnerable to the risk of blitzkrieg operations from the preponderant in-place formations of the Warsaw Pact.

Understandably, in advance of a General Election, there is little political incentive for reform. The electoral risks of seeking to match commitments, strategy and equipment more closely to resources outweigh the military benefits. After an election, however, there is no excuse for inaction. The sheer volume of essential equipments and their cost, Eurofighter, Harrier GR5, Tornado F3, Type 23 Frigates, EH101 helicopters, additional armour and above all Trident D5, all to be paid for from a budget no longer growing in real terms, while retaining expensive and professional Armed Forces, means that however much immobility in defence planning is made a political virtue – a change in Britain's strategy and military posture is inevitable.

In the post General Election review, the most compelling impetus for change should be strategic and not merely the familiar postwar economic need to save money on Britain's national defence. Unlike previous British defence reviews, which were unilateral *fait accomplis*, the eventual but inevitable reappraisal of the United Kingdom's defence commitments, plans and programmes must take place in the context of a multilateral re-examination of national rôles and responsibilities within the NATO Alliance as a whole, set against Britain's social and economic circumstances and national security priorities.

In the course of the analysis and prescriptions of earlier pages it has become clear that Britain must remain an independent nuclear power through the acquisition and deployment of the Trident D5 submarine-launched ballistic missile system. The retention by the Royal Navy, however, of its supreme responsibility as the custodian of Britain's national strategic nuclear deterrent, must not be allowed to interfere with the overdue process of restoring the United Kingdom's maritime power. Britain's geography, history, traditions, trade and global influence predispose her to maritime greatness. Its restoration in the fullest sense is a worthy national objective.

Mobility, flexibility and the ability to project and concentrate military power rapidly, if necessary at considerable distance from British shores should be the hallmarks of the United Kingdom's contribution to NATO as the turn of the century approaches. These characteristics put a premium on sea and airpower, as well as on the highest standards of equipment and training in all three Services.

Preserving the peace is a highly uncertain and unpredictable process in as much as actual threats of conflict are often most likely in the least expected places. Versatility, multi-rôle capability and adaptability are essential for Britain's Armed Forces if the British people are to obtain good value for the money spent on their defence. By agreement, and over a reasonable timescale, the fixed static role of the British Army of the Rhine should be greatly diminished. The ability of the United Kingdom rapidly to reinforce NATO forces on the continent of Europe by sea and air, particularly with offensive air power must be substantially increased. On land the premier power among the European members of the NATO military organisation is the Federal Republic of Germany. She should accordingly assume command of the Northern Army Group in place of Britain.

In the future conflicts could be prolonged if deterrence fails. The Northern Ireland experience has demonstrated that even low intensity operations can be extremely protracted. The Iran/Iraq war has made plain that long conventional wars of attrition can still be fought. Furthermore if the Federal Republic of Germany refuses to assume a greater responsbility for its own defence in the Northern Army Group area, the need to maintain an expensive and manpower intensive force of 55,000 men in Germany would continue, perpetuating the rigidities and imbalance in Britain's defence posture.

Whether or not political agreement can be reached on a new rôle in

NATO for the United Kingdom which incorporates a reduction in the numbers of British troops deployed in West Germany, new manpower policies will be needed for the armed forces based on a core of professional regulars supplemented by less expensive personnel engaged for a shorter period, and larger Reserves. Without new policies the costs of maintaining armed forces of adequate size for national security and for an appropriate contribution to the defence of the NATO area will become an unacceptable burden on the defence budget.

Both for social and military reasons the All-Party political taboo on any serious discussion of the merits of national service must be lifted. A political directive should be issued to the Defence, Employment, Education and Social Security Ministries instructing them to examine the full implications of a reintroduction of military national service in Britain.

As well as furthering the desirable social objective of greater public participation in national defence, the reintroduction of National Service would provide young men with a training at least as valuable technically as that offered by the Youth Training Scheme (YTS) and in character formation, discipline, comradeship and responsibility one which could be made infinitely more rewarding. For the Services it would provide the new source of manpower which they need as well as a steady flow of trained reservists.

Lastly, the British people must be reawakened to the fact of Britain's military weakness in face of a growing Soviet threat. Decisive political leadership will be required in Government, Parliament and the community to generate the popular support required to sustain the overdue improvements in Britain's defences proposed in this book. A sudden clarion call to arms is not required so much as a steady note of encouragement for reform, revitalisation and rationalisation of Britain's defence efforts.

Notes

CHAPTER 1

1. *Labour in Power, 1945–51*, by Kenneth O. Morgan, Oxford University Press, London 1985, p. 257.
2. Morgan, op. cit., p. 274.
3. *Attlee*, by Kenneth Harris, Weidenfeld & Nicolson, London 1982, p. 288.
4. Morgan, op. cit., p. 279.
5. *History of the Second World War. Grand Strategy Vol. VI*, by John Ehrman, HMSO, London, 1956.
6. Morgan, op. cit., p. 435.
7. *Defence. Outline of Future Policy*. Cmnd. 124, para. 24, April 1957.
8. Contrast these figures with those for 1986–87. Once again, Britain appears to be over-reaching itself with a higher proportion of its GDP (5.2 per cent) spend on defence than any other nation, except USSR (12 per cent), USA (6.9 per cent) and Greece (7.1 per cent). The latter can perhaps be regarded as a "special case".
9. *Hansard, Vol. 707, No. 69, 3 March, 1965, cols. 1329, 1341*. Mr. Denis Healey, Secretary of State for Defence.
10. *Statement on the Defence Estimates (SDE), 1966. Cmnd 2902, Part II, Annex H.*
11. See *The Uncertain Ally, British Defence Policy 1960–90*, by Michael Chichester and John Wilkinson, Gower Publishing Co., Aldershot, 1982. Ch. 3.
12. *Hansard, 16 December 1964, cols. 423–424*. Mr. Harold Wilson, Prime Minister.
13 *Hansard, Vol. 707, No. 69, 3 March 1965, col. 1337*, Mr. Denis Healey.
14. *SDE 1967. Cmnd 3203, para. 15.*
15. *Statement on Public Expenditure 1968–70. Cmnd 3515, January 1968.*
16. *SDE 1968, Cmnd 3540, para. 3a.*
17. *Supplementary Statement on Defence Policy 1970. Cmd 4251, October 1970, para. 2(3).*
18. *The Labour Party Manifesto, February 1974, p. 14.*
19. *Hansard, Vol. 891, No. 119, 6 May 1975, col. 1288*. Mr. Roy Mason, Secretary of State for Defence.
20. *SDE 1975, Cmnd 5976, Ch. I. para. 45.*
21. *Hansard, Vol. 891, No. 119, 6 May 1975, col. 1230*. Mr. Roy Mason.
22. *Hansard, Vol. 891, No. 119, 6 May 1975, col. 1235*, Mr. Roy Mason.
23. *SDE 1975, Cmnd 5976, Ch. I, para. 25.*
24. *SDE 1986, Cmnd 9763–I, p. 7. "The Seamless Robe".*
25. *The Times, 26 February 1976.*
26. *Hansard, Vol. 988, No. 213, 15 July 1980, col. 1236*, Mr. Francis Pym, Secretary of State for Defence.
27. *The United Kingdom Defence Programme. The Way Forward, Cmnd 8288, June 1981.*
28. *Hansard, Vol. 7, No. 128, 25 June 1981, col. 387*, Mr. John Nott, Secretary of State for Defence.
29. *Hansard, Vol. 8, No. 137, 8 July 1981, col. 276*, Mr. John Nott.
30. *Cmnd 8288, para. 16.*
31. *SDE 1986, Cmnd 9763–I, p. 40, para. 503.*
32. *House of Commons. Second Report from the Defence Committee Session 1985–86. Statement on the Defence Estimates 1986. June 1986, pp. 163–4.*

33. *Hansard, Vol. 100, No. 140, 1 July 1986, col. 852*, Mr. John Lee, Parliamentary Under-Secretary of State for Defence Procurement.
34. *Hansard, Vol. 62, No. 174, 19 June 1984, col. 176*, Mr. John Stanley, Minister of State for the Armed Forces.
35. In a closely argued Memorandum to the House of Commons Defence Committee in 1981, this respected defence economist concluded that either "*an across-the-board dilution and degradation of the forces' ability to discharge their responsibilities, or an unplanned, almost fortuitous, assumption of the kind of unbalanced force structure that has been discussed*" would be the result of such an attempt. In 1986 the latter seemed to be taking place.
36. *SDE 1986, Cmnd 9763–I, p. 41.*
37. *SDE 1986, Cmnd 9763–II, Relevant Tables.*
38. *Hansard, Vol. 100, No. 139, 30 June 1986, cols. 710–712*, Mr. George Younger, Secretary of State for Defence.
39. *Hansard, Vol. 100, No. 139, 30 June 1986, col. 713*, Mr. George Younger.
40. *House of Commons, Second Report from the Defence Committee Session 1985–86. Statement on the Defence Estimates 1986, June 1986, pp. xvii–xviii.*

CHAPTER III

1. *Hansard, Vol. 105, No. 1, 12 November 1986, col. 24.*
2. *Hansard, Vol. 105, No. 1, 12 November 1986, col. 23.*
3. Journal of the Royal United Services Institute for Defence Studies, June 1985, pp. 3–8. The lecture was entitled *Defence and Security in the Nuclear Age*. It was a classic example of Foreign Office obfuscation, all in the interrogative mode.
4. British Prime Minister's Press Conference, Washington, USA, 15 November 1986.
5. *House of Lords Hansard, Vol. 482, No. 2, 13 November 1986.*
6. *Hansard, Vol. 482, No. 2, 13 November 1986.*
7. *Hansard, Vol. 482, No. 2, 13 November 1986, col. 99.*
8. *Hansard, Vol. 105, No. 1, 12 November 1986, col. 23.*

CHAPTER IV

1. *Education in the Armed Forces*. A Report of a Seminar held at the Royal United Services Institute for Defence Studies on Wednesday, 15 November 1972, p. 3, published by RUSI, Whitehall, London SW1. (February 1973.)
2. *Ibid, p. 4.*

CHAPTER V

1. "*The Russians dash on towards that thin red line tipped with steel.*" Sir William Howard Russell, *The British Expedition to the Crimea*, (1877), p. 156.
2. *Hansard Vol. 92, no. 66, 26 February 1986, col. 969*. Mr. Kevin McNamara.
3. *SDE 1986, Cmnd 9763–I Ch. 4, para. 439.*
4. *Hansard, Vol. 68, No. 18, 29 November 1984*, Mr. John Stanley Minister of State for the Armed Forces.
5. Report in *The Times*, 28 February 1985.
6. *The Times, 15 August 1968*. Before his tragically early death in 1985, Charles Douglas-Home had become Editor of the paper. In the following year a collection of his writings on defence and other issues was published in "*No End of a Lesson. Leading Articles from* The Times *under Charles Douglas-Home*". Alliance Publishers for the Institute for European Defence and Strategic Studies, London 1986.
7. *The Times*, 23 May 1982.
8. *Hansard, Vol. 92, No. 66, 26 February 1986*. Mr. John Wilkinson.
9. Quoted in an article in the *Sunday Telegraph*, 28 September 1986.
10. *Attlee, op. cit., p. 323.*
11. *SDE 1986, Cmnd 9763–I Ch. 6, para. 632.*
12. Quoted in a Letter to *The Times* 7 July 1986.
13. See "*The Uncertain Ally*" *op. cit., Ch. 17*. This remains the only published study of a

subject which is anathema to the regulars, disliked by the Whitehall establishment and said to be frowned upon by Prime Minister Thatcher. It is seldom discussed by defence correspondents who regard it as a somewhat mundane subject compared with the newsworthiness of nuclear policy, SDI, or the latest procurement foul-up.

14. *Hansard, Vol. 90, No. 47, 30 January 1986, col. 1171.* Mr. Robert Key.
15. *Hansard, Vol. 91, No. 52, 6 February 1986, Col. 1529.* Mr. John Lee, Under Secretary of State for Defence Procurement.
16. *House of Commons Second Report from the Defence Committee Session 1985–86, Statement on the Defence Estimates 1986, p. xvii, para. 55.*
17. *The Uncertain Ally op. cit., pp. 193–203.*
18. "*Defence Policy.*" The Adam Smith Institute Omega Report, ASI (Research) Ltd, London, 1983.
    The Adam Smith Institute's OMEGA Project was conceived to fill a significant gap in the field of policy research, to develop new policy initiatives, to research them, and issue them for public discussion. A number of the Defence Report's suggestions were subsequently adopted by the Defence Ministry, notably in connection with competitive tendering. Altogether twenty reports on different aspects of government concern were published collectively in *The Omega File* in 1985.
19. This politically important field has been cultivated by the former Conservative Minister, David Howell, in *Blind Victory, A Study in Income, Wealth and Power*, Hamish Hamilton, London, 1986.
20. *The Omega Defence Report, op. cit., p. 38.*

CHAPTER VI

1. Press Notice No. 20/86 of the National Audit Office issued 12 August 1986.
2. Second Report from the Defence Select Committee Session 1981–82 on Ministry of Defence Organisation and Procurement, p. xxvii.
3. *Ibid*, p. 410.
4. Letter to *The Times* of 7 January 1987, " *'Sloth' in Weapons-Buying System*", by Kenneth Warren MP.
5. Second Report from the Select Committee on Defence as above, p. 410.
6. *The Times*, 13 August 1986. Article by Sheila Gunn of London.
7. For two analyses which put the Westland crisis in context see *European Helicopters for the 1990s*. Report of the Assembly of WEU, 3 November 1986, by John Wilkinson MP.
8. *A European Earth Resources Detection Satellite Programme*. Report by John Wilkinson MP. Assembly of WEU. Document 842, 29 April 1980.

CHAPTER VII

1. Senator Gary Hart. Interview in the *Sunday Times*. London, 16 November 1986.
2. *Is Deterrence Dead*? by Dr. Harlank Ullman, RUSI Journal of the Royal United Services Institute for Defence Studies, London, September 1985.
3. Feature article on the Common Agricultural Policy. *The Times*, London, 24 November 1986.
4. Leading article. *The Times*, London, 18 June 1984.
5. *The Uncertain Ally*. op. cit. Ch. 13.
6. The Roth-Glenn-Nunn Amendment on NATO Defence Industrial Co-operation was approved by the United States Senate by 87 votes to 1 on 13 May 1982. Its principal proposal is that the NATO Allies of the USA join with it in agreeing to co-ordinate more effectively their defence efforts and resources to create, at acceptable costs, a credible, collective, conventional force for the defence of the North Atlantic Treaty area.
7. Leading article *The Times*, London, 23 April 1986.
8. Report in *The Times*, London, 16 January 1986. See also *France–Allemagne: Une Synergie Nouvelle. Le Monde*, Paris, 21 May 1986.
9. The 1948 Brussels Treaty between the United Kingdom, France and the Benelux countries established Western European Union as a preliminary to the formation of a European Defence Community (EDC). When the attempt to form EDC finally failed in 1954, the

Paris Agreements of that year enlarged WEU to include Italy and the Federal Republic of Germany, thus establishing the seven-nation membership which remains to this day. The Agreements included the setting up of a Council and a Parliamentary Assembly for WEU. Inevitably, its work in the field of European defence coordination became overshadowed by the larger and more influential machinery of NATO.

See also *Relaunching Western European Union. Implications for the Atlantic Alliance*, by Alfred Cohen, Secretary General of WEU. NATO Review No. 4, August 1986.

10. Extract from the English text of M. Chirac's speech to the WEU Assembly in Paris, 2 December 1986.
11. Ditto as (10).
12. *Flexible Response – Is There An Alternative?* by Vice Admiral J. R. Oswald and Wing Commander R. McKendrick. Journal of the RUSI for Defence Studies, London, March 1986.
13. For an interesting discussion on the need for Europe to adopt a wider strategic perspective see *"ORBIS", Fall 1981, "The Soviet Global Theatre and the West"*, by Pierre M. Gallois. *"This is the menace now weighing on what remains of the free world, this clouding of the mind by a few hundred kilometres of frontiers in Europe, while the fate of Europe is at stake daily in Africa and Asia"*.
14. *Race to the Swift*. op. cit., p. 76.
15. Ibid, p. 288.
16. *Britain's Naval Future*, by (Sir) James Cable. The Macmillan Press. London 1983, p. 185.

CHAPTER VIII

1. *Hansard, Vol. 62, No. 173, col. 141, 18 June 1984*. Mr. Michael Heseltine, Secretary of State for Defence.
2. *Hansard, Vol. 80, No. 132, col. 1914, 12 June 1985*. Mr. Michael Heseltine.
3. House of Commons. Second Report from the Defence Committee Session 1985–86. *Statement on the Defence Estimates 1986, p. xvi*.
4. *The Way Forward*, op.cit, para. 16.
5. A principle laid down by the Prime Minister, Mrs. Margaret Thatcher, prior to the announcement that Boeing had won the AWACS contract.
6. *The Times*, London, 22 December 1986.
7. *Race to the Swift*, op. cit., p. 245.
8. *The Military Balance 1986–87*, IISS, London 1986.
9. *The Times*, London, 23 April 1985.
10. *The British Way in Warfare Revisited*, by Hew Strachan, *The Historical Journal*, Vol. 26, 2 June 1983. Cambridge University Press.

    In one of the few debates on defence policy in the House of Lords, a Field Marshal in a speech supporting the conclusions of *The Way Forward* praised the government for its determination not to be swept off the course set by the Review "by the waves of post-imperial and naval nostalgia" which had affected public opinion in the aftermath of the Falklands campaign. (*House of Lords Official Report Vol. 434, No. 133, col. 171, 27 July 1982*.)
11. Government White Paper, *The Central Organisation for Defence*, Cmnd. 9315, July 1984.

Index